UNIX System V Commands:
Programmer's Rapid Reference

UNIX System V Commands: Programmer's Rapid Reference

Baird Peterson, Ph.D.

VAN NOSTRAND REINHOLD
New York

Copyright © 1992 by Van Nostrand Reinhold
Library of Congress Catalog Card Number 90-19999
ISBN 0-442-00998-4

Manufactured in the United States of America

Published by Van Nostrand Reinhold
115 Fifth Avenue
New York, New York 10003

Chapman and Hall
2-6 Boundary Row
London, SE1 8HN, England

Thomas Nelson Australia
102 Dodds Street
South Melbourne 3205
Victoria, Australia

Nelson Canada
1120 Birchmount Road
Scarborough, Ontario M1K 5G4, Canada

16 15 14 13 12 11 10 9 8 7 6 5 4 3 2 1

Library of Congress Cataloging-in-Publication Data
Peterson, Baird.
    UNIX system V commands : programmer's rapid reference / Baird
Peterson.
    p.   cm.
    Includes bibliographical references and index.
    ISBN 0-442-00998-4
    1. UNIX (Computer operating system)   I. Title.
QA76.76.063P525   1991   90-19999
005.4'3--dc20   CIP

*to Maureen, Colin,
and my mother*

Contents

Preface

This book was written to help two different kinds of readers: newcomers to UNIX System V Release 4 and experienced UNIX System V Release 4 programmers. The book has features that help newcomers find descriptions of UNIX software development commands quickly without having to know the names of the commands. Also, the descriptions of UNIX features are organized to reduce reading time, something that both kinds of readers will enjoy.

UNIX has hundreds of commands, system calls, library routines, and file formats. This book presents descriptions of commands for UNIX System V that are of interest in general software development. The commands covered include all AT&T System V commands for general software development.

Acknowledgments

Many people helped to create this book. I thank my literary agent, Bill Gladstone of Waterside Productions, Inc. I also thank the people at Van Nostrand Reinhold for their editorial support, especially my acquisition editor, Dianne Littwin; managing editor, Alberta Gordon; editorial assistants Marybeth Lorenc and Robert Gasperi; and my developmental editor, Paul Sobel. I thank my anonymous reviewers for helping to make this a better book. I thank Adele Just for her excellent editorial help. I thank my wife Maureen for her constant support and encouragement.

INTRODUCTION

Notation

The following kinds of notation are used in this book.

`constant width type` denotes user input such as commands, options, arguments, variable names, and the names of directories.

`command` (`[name year[letter]|letter(s)]`) refers to a book or to a section of this book where a description of the specified `command` may be found. The form

$$\text{command } (letter(s))$$

refers to a description in Part 1 [`command` (CP)] or Part 2 [`command` (F)] of the present book. The form

$$\text{command } (name \; year[letter])$$

gives the author `name` of a book listed in the Bibliograpy of this book, the `year` the book was published, and the specific book (`letter`) published that `year` if the author had more than one book published in that year. For example,

$$\text{directory } (Peterson \; 1992a)$$

refers to a description of the `directory` function in a book published by Peterson in 1992.

`italic constant width type` denotes the names of variables to which specific values must be assigned.

$<>$ indicates input that is not displayed on the screen when it is typed, for example, passwords, tabs, or RETURN. Such input appears between angle brackets. The angle brackets themselves are not input.

$<\hat{}char>$ indicates control characters. The circumflex ($\hat{}$) denotes the control key (CTRL), while *char* denotes some key. For example, $<\hat{}d>$ denotes the value obtained by holding the control key down and striking the D key. The letter D is not displayed, and the angle brackets themselves are not input.

[] indicates optional arguments and command options. One or more of the options enclosed by the brackets (but not the brackets themselves) are input.

| separates optional arguments in cases where only one of two listed options may be chosen. For example, in the following command:

1

$$\text{command } [\,arg1|arg2\,]$$

either *arg1* or *arg2* may be chosen, but not both.

. . . means that more than one argument like the preceding argument may be used on a command line.

How to Use This Book

If you are an experienced UNIX programmer and you already know all the names of the UNIX commands and system calls, see Part I for the command description you seek. The descriptive entries are given in alphabetical order.

If you are a newcomer to UNIX programming, read the following section.

Classification of UNIX System V Commands

If you don't know the names of all the UNIX commands used for software development, turn to page 5 to read the section that classifies UNIX commands.

Part I

UNIX Commands

This chapter consists of three main parts:

- An explanation of the format of the entries that describe UNIX commands.
- A command classification table (page 5) that helps you quickly find the appropriate command for your purpose.
- The descriptive entries themselves in alphabetical order.

Each descriptive entry consist of up to six separate sections: Name, Synopsis, Description, Options and Arguments, Files, and See Also.

Name

The name of each command is followed by a brief phrase describing its purpose.

Synopsis

The synopsis shows a command and any options and arguments that it accepts according to the following syntax:

3

command [*option*(s)] [*commandarg*(s)]

where

command specifies an executable file.
option is either - *argletternoopt*(s) or
- *argletter optionarg*

where

argletternoopt, a single letter, represents an option that requires
no option argument,
argletter, a single letter, represents an option that requires an option
argument, followed by optional spaces, and
optionarg is a character string specifying an argument for the previous
argletter.
commandarg(s) is "-" by itself, indicating standard input, or is a path
name or other command argument that does not begin with "-".

Description
Each description contains general details about the command.

Options and Arguments
Where possible (and it nearly always is), all of the information about each
argument of a command is put in this subsection. The descriptions of arguments
are sorted in ASCII order of the argument names as these are given in the
synopsis, except that when an argument is preceded by a " + " it is grouped with
other arguments that are preceded by "-". Usually, when information about an
argument must appear in other subsections or in the material about another
argument, the argument description will point to such material.

Files
In general, this section describes various files and directories used by the
command. Several descriptive entries refer to BINDIR, INCDIR, LIBDIR,
LLIBDIR, and TMPDIR. These five names represent directory names whose
actual values are specified where necessary.

See Also
This section points to related commands or other sources of additional information.

class (CP)   Command Classification   class (CP)

This section classifies the System V Release 4 commands described in this book.

Software Generation Utilities for Various Languages

Macro Preprocessing

Object File Manipulation

Profiling

Software Version Control

Sorting

C Programming Utilities

C Compilation

C Debugging Aids

---

admin (CP)   SOURCE CODE CONTROL SYSTEM   admin (CP)

Name

admin—create SCCS files or alter SCCS file parameters.

Synopsis

admin   [-n]   [-i[*filename*]]   [-rre*l*]   [-t[*filename*]]
[-f*flag*[*flagval*]] [-d*flag*[*flagval*]] [-a*login*] [-e*login*]
[-m[*mrlist*]] [-y[*comment*]] [-h] [-z] *files*

Description

admin   creates new SCCS s-files (see below) or changes parameters of
existing SCCS s-files. Text controlled by SCCS must be interpretable by the
standard UNIX editors (ed and vi). Files named by admin are created if they
do not exist. SCCS file parameters are initialized as specified by arguments of
the command. If no initial value is specified for an argument, a default value is
assigned. If a file specified by admin already exists, parameters specified by
admin are changed; other parameters remain the same.

When a directory is named in admin, each file in the directory is processed
by admin, except that non-SCCS files and unreadable files are ignored. If −
is given as the name following the −i argument, each line of standard input is
taken to be the name of an SCCS file to be processed by admin; non-SCCS
files and unreadable files are ignored.

The admin command uses a transient lock file (z.file-name) to prevent
simultaneous updates of an SCCS file by different users [see get (CP) for
additional details].

The last component of any SCCS file name must have the form s.*filename*.

Newly created SCCS files are assigned mode 444 [chmod (Peterson 1991a)].
Any writing by admin is sent to a temporary file, x.file-name [see get (CP)].
The temporary file is created with the same mode as the SCCS file if the SCCS
file already exists or with mode 444 if a new SCCS file is being created. If
admin executes successfully, the SCCS file is deleted and x.*filename* is
renamed with the name of the SCCS file. Thus an SCCS file is modified only
if no errors occurred.

Any directories containing SCCS files should have mode 755. The mode of
the directories prevents anyone except the owner from changing SCCS files
contained in the directories. The mode of the SCCS files prevents any changes
except by using SCCS commands.

The mode of an SCCS file should be changed to 644 if the file must be
patched. This allows ed to be used. After editing, use admin −h to examine
the file for corruption. Next, execute admin −z to compute a proper checksum.
Finally, execute admin −h again to ensure that the SCCS file is valid.

Options and Arguments

Arguments to admin may appear in any order. These arguments consist of
keyletter arguments beginning with a hyphen (−) or file names. The effects of
each argument apply independently to each specified file.

-a*login* specifies a login name or a numerical UNIX system group ID to be added to the list of users authorized to make changes (deltas) to the SCCS file. More than one -a keyletter may be used on the command line of a single admin command. Also, the list may simultaneously have as many *logins* or group IDs as desired. Specifying a group ID has the effect of specifying all of the login names common to that group ID. Anyone may add deltas if no list of users is specified. If ! precedes a *login* or group ID, the login or group ID is refused permission to make deltas.

-d*flag* deletes the specified *flag* from an SCCS file. More than one -d keyletter may be used on the command line of an admin command. The -d keyletter can only be specified for an SCCS file that already exists. See -f keyletter for permissible *flag* names.

l*list* gives a *list* of releases to be unlocked. See documentation for the -f keyletter for the syntax of *list* and for a description of l.

-e*login* deletes a login name or numerical group ID from the list of users allowed to make deltas (changes) to an SCCS file. More than one -e keyletter may be used on the command line of a single admin command. Specifying a group ID deletes all of the *login* names common to that group ID.

-f*flag*[*flagval*] specifies a flag and, optionally, a value, *flagval*, to be placed in the SCCS file. More than one -f may appear on the command line of a single admin command. The flags and their permissible values are as follows:

b lets the get (CP) command create branch deltas. See the -b keyletter of get (CP).

c*ceil* sets the highest release number (ceiling) which may be retrieved by a get (CP) command for editing. The ceiling must be greater than 0 but less than or equal to 9999. The default is 9999 when c is not specified.

d*SID* sets the default SCCS Identification string (SID) number used by a get (CP) command. See delta (CP) for the definition of SID number.

f*floor* sets a minimum value, *floor*, for the number of the release which may be retrieved by a get (CP) command for editing. The *floor* must be greater than 0 but less than or equal to 9999. The default is 1 when f is unspecified.

i[*string*] treats the "No id keywords (ge6)" message issued by get (CP) or delta (CP) as a fatal error. (The message is issued when SCCS identification keywords are not found in text stored or retrieved in an SCCS file.) Otherwise, the message is treated as a warning. If *string* is supplied, it must match the keywords. The *string* argument can contain keywords but not newlines.

j allows concurrent updates to the same version of an s-file. This option can cause file corruption if it is used carelessly.

llist lists releases for which deltas are no longer allowed. The *list* has syntax as follows:

$$<list> ::= <range> \mid <list>, <range>$$
$$<range> ::= RELEASE\ NUMBER \mid a$$

Putting a in *list* specifies all releases of the named file. The get −e command fails when used with one of the releases specified in *list*.

m*module* gives the module name of the SCCS file to be substituted for all occurrences of the %M% keyword in the SCCS file text retrieved by get (CP). The default value of *module* if m is not specified is the name of the SCCS file with the leading s deleted.

n makes delta (CP) create a "null" delta for each release that is to be skipped when a delta is made in a new release. Branch deltas can be created by using these null deltas. If n is not specified, any releases skipped no longer exist in the SCCS file. No branch delta can later be created from such a release.

q*text* specifies text to be substituted wherever the %Q% keyword occurs in an SCCS file gotten by get.

t*type* specifies the type of module in the SCCS file substituted wherever the %Y% keyword occurs in SCCS file text gotten by get (CP).

v*pgm* makes delta ask for Modification Request (MR) numbers as the reason for making a delta. If v*pgm* is used when an SCCS file is being created, the m keyletter must be used too, even if its value is null. The optional value, *pgm*, gives the name of an optional validity checking program for MR numbers. The program receives the module name, the value of −t*type*, and the value of −m[*mrlist*].

−h checks the structure of an s-file and compares a newly computed checksum with a checksum stored in the first line of the file. The checksum is the sum of all of the characters in the SCCS file except the characters in the first line of the SCCS file. This keyletter prevents writing to the file.

−i[*filename*] gives the *filename* of the file from which to take text for a new SCCS file. The text is the first delta of the file. Only one SCCS file may be created by admin if −i is used. If −i is omitted, the SCCS file is created empty. If a single admin command is used to create more than one SCCS file, the files must be created empty, i.e., −i must not be used. If i is used, −n also must be used. If −i is used but *name* is omitted, text is gotten by reading the standard input until an EOF is found.

−m[*mrlist*] inserts an *mrlist* of MR numbers into the SCCS s-file as a reason for creating the initial delta in the same fashion as delta (CP). If −m[mrlist] is set, the −v *flag* also must be set, and *flag* must be the name of a program that validates MR numbers. If the −v *flag* is not set or validation of MR numbers fails, admin issues error messages.

−n creates a new SCCS s-file.

−rrel gives the initial release number for a new s-file. The initial release is 1 if −r is not used. −rrel may be used only if −i also is used. The level of any initial delta is always 1. Initial deltas are named 1.1 by default.

−t[filename] specifies the file from which to take descriptive text for the SCCS a-file. The filename must also be given if the −i and/or the −n files are specified (admin is creating a new SCCS s-file) and the −t letter is used. For SCCS files that already exist, descriptive text (if any) is removed if −t is supplied but no filename is supplied. If both −t and a filename are supplied, text (if any) replaces the text (if any) currently in the existing SCCS file.

−y[comment] puts comment text into the SCCS file as a comment for the initial delta in the same fashion as delta (CP). This argument is valid only if −i or −n is used, i.e., a new SCCS file is being created. The default when −y is not specified is insertion of a comment line: "date and time created YY/MM/DD HH:MM:SS by login."

−z recomputes the SCCS s-file checksum and stores it in the first line of the SCCS s-file (see −h above). Using −z on a corrupted file may prevent detection of the file corruption.

files specifies s-files which are to be created or which already exist and are to be modified.

Files

See get (CP) for additional details about SCCS files.

d-file is a temporary copy of the g-file, created during delta execution and deleted afterward.

g-file contains changes to be made to an original s-file. It exists before delta execution and is gone after delta execution is complete.

p-file contains the SCCS Identification string (SID) of the file being updated, the next SID when the g-file is restored to the s-file, and the login of the user retrieving the g-file. It exists before delta execution and may remain afterward.

q-file is used by delta when it is updating a p-file. It is created during delta execution and deleted afterward.

s-file is the primary SCCS file, holding the original file and deltas to it.

/usr/bin/bdiff computes differences between g-file and the gotten file.

x-file is created whenever changes are made to an s-file. All actual changes are made to the x-file, holding the sfile safe in case of a crash. The existing s-file is replaced by the x-file when changes are finished.

z-file is a lock file that prevents simultaneous s-file updates by different users. It contains the process ID of the currently executing SCCS process.

See Also

bdiff (AT&T 1990q), cdc (CP), comb (CP), delta (CP), ed (AT&T 1990q), get (CP), help (CP), prs (CP), rmdel (CP), sact (CP), sccsdiff (CP), unget (CP), val (CP), vc (CP), what (CP)

ar (CP)	LIBRARY MANAGEMENT	ar (CP)

Name

ar—maintain archive files

Synopsis

ar [-V] -key [keyarg] [positname] archfile [name . . .]

Description

ar maintains groups of files that are combined into one archive file for use as a library by the link editor and various compilers. The command can combine several files into one archive file. Text file archives created by ar are portable between all implementations of System V.

At the beginning of each archive file is a magic number [see ar (F)] consisting of printable ASCII characters. The magic number is followed by constituent files, each file being preceded by a header [see ar (F)] that also consists of printable ASCII characters. Thus, the entire archive is printable if the archive is composed of printable files.

An archive symbol table [see ar (F)] is generated when the ar command is used to update or create an archive if the archive contains at least one object file. Also, the s option (see below) forces the symbol table to be rebuilt. If created, the symbol table is put in a specially named file that is always the first file in the archive. This specially named file is not accessible to the user. The link editor, ld (CP), uses the archive symbol table to make efficient multiple passes over libraries of object files.

Options and Arguments

-V causes ar to print its version number on stderr.

The operation of the ar command also is determined by a command key and by command options. The command key, key, is a mandatory part of the command line. It may begin with a hyphen. It consists of one of the letters dmpqrtx, described below:

Command Keys

d removes the named files from the archive file.

m is a positioning character that moves the named files to the end of the archive. The *positname* argument must be present when a positioning character is present. As in r, it must tell where the files are to be moved.

p prints the named files in the archive.

q quickly appends the specified files to the end of the archive. Optional positioning characters a, b, and i are not valid. No checking is done to determine whether added files are already in the archive. The q option avoids quadratic behavior in building a large archive file by file.

r replaces specified files in the archive. If the *keyarg*, u, is used with r, archive files are replaced only when they have modification dates earlier than the modification dates of replacement files. New files are placed at the end of the archive unless key arguments a, b, or i are used with r. See entries for a, b, and i below.

t prints a table showing the contents of the archive file. The names of all files in the archive are put in the table if no names are specified. Otherwise only the names given are tabled.

x extracts the specified files. All files are extracted if no names are given. The x argument never modifies a file.

Command Options

One or more of the following key arguments may be used in combination:

a specifies the file position after *positname*. The *positname* argument must be present if a is used.

b specifies the file position before *positname*; the *positname* argument must be present if b is used.

c suppresses the default message produced when *archfile* is created.

i specifies the file position before *positname*; the *positname* argument must be present if i is used.

l is an obsolete option that formerly was used to put temporary files in the current working (local) directory instead of in TMPDIR, the default temporary directory. l is now recognized and ignored. It will be removed from the next release.

s forces rebuilding of the archive symbol table even when ar (CP) is invoked with a command that will modify the contents of the archive. The s option can restore an archive after the strip (CP) command is used.

u when used with r, causes replacement only for those files with modification dates later than the modification dates of corresponding files in the archive.

v gives a verbose file-by-file report of the generation of a new archive file from an old archive file and constituent files. A long listing of all information about files is given if **t** is used with **v**. Each file must be preceded by a name if **x** is used with **v**.

archfile is the name of the archive. Archive names are suffixed with **.a**.

name specifies the names of files in the archive file. If the same filename is given twice in the argument list, the file may be put in the archive twice.

positname is the file that is used as a reference point when other files are positioned in the archive.

Files

$TMPDIR/* contains temporary files

See Also

ld (CP), **lorder** (CP), **nm** (CP), **strip** (CP), **tsort** (CP), **a.out** (F), **ar** (F), **tmpnam** (Peterson 1992a)

as (CP)	ASSEMBLY/DISASSEMBLY	as (CP)

Name

as—assemble named file; place result in **a.out**

Synopsis

as [*option*(s)] *filename*

Description

as reads an assembly language source program and generates an object file that contains binary code and relocation information that is ready to be processed by the linker/loader. The assembler should be accessed through a compilation interface program such as **cc** (CP).

There may be only one forward-referenced symbol per arithmetic expression. Keywords for **m4** (CP) cannot be used as symbols (functions, labels, or variables) in the input file if the **m4** option, **−m**, is used because in this case **m4** cannot tell which are assembler symbols and which are macros. Finally, the **.align** assembler directive may not work correctly in the **text** section when long/short address optimization is specified.

Options and Arguments

The option flags may be specified in any order:

−dl is an obsolete option that was formerly used to suppress line number information in the object file. The assembler now issues a warning when it encounters this option.

−m executes the m4 (CP) macro processor on assembler input.

−n turns off short/long address optimization. The default is that optimization occurs.

−o *objfile* puts assembly output in *objfile*. The default output file name is formed by deleting the .s suffix, if it exists, and appending an .o suffix.

−Q{y|n} puts the version number of the currently executing assembler in the object file if −Qy is specified. The default option, −Qn, does not put the version number in the file.

−R unlinks (deletes) the input file after assembly is done.

−T makes as accept obsolete assembler directives.

−V writes the assembler version number on the standard error output.

−Y[md],*direct* gets the file of predefined macros (d) and/or the m4 pre-processor (m) from directory *direct*.

filename is the file containing assembly code to be assembled.

Files

/var/tmp contains temporary files. The location of the temporary file can be redefined by changing the TMPDIR environment variable [see tmpnam (Peterson 1992a)].

See Also

cc (CP), ld (CP), m4 (CP), nm (CP), strip (CP), a.out (F), tmpnam (Peterson 1992a)

---

cb (CP)   **C DEBUGGING AIDS**   **cb (CP)**

Name

cb—C program beautifier

Synopsis

[cb [−s] [−j] [−l *length*] [*filename* . . .]

Description

cb reads syntactically correct C code from the specified file(s) or from standard input and writes the code to the standard output after formatting it with
spacing and indentation to display its structure. If no command line options are
given, the specified files are structured so that braces align vertically and code
within braces is indented one tab stop. Any punctuation hidden in preprocessor
statements will cause indentation errors.

cb preserves the format of structure initializations. It also preserves all user
newlines by default.

Options and Arguments

-j rejoins lines that have been split.

−l *length* splits lines that are longer than *length*.

−s standardizes the style of code to be as it is in *The C Programming
Language* by Kernighan and Ritchie.

−V causes cb to print its version number on stderr.

filename is the file containing C programs to be beautified. Several files
may be specified.

See Also

cc (CP)

---

cc (CP)   C COMPILATION   cc (CP)

Name

cc—C compiler

Synopsis

[cc [*arguments*] *filenames*

Description

cc is the interface of the C Compilation System, a set of tools consisting of
a preprocessor, compiler, optimizer, assembler, basic block analyzer, and link
editor. cc accepts options, processes them, and executes the appropriate tools
after passing them the proper arguments.

The arguments to cc may consist of those given in the section below, plus
the names of C-compatible object programs. These latter arguments, if any,
name object programs found in libraries of C-compatible routines or in files

produced by earlier execution(s) of cc. Object programs produced by previous executions of cc, library routines, and the results of the current execution of cc are linked (in the specified order) to generate an executable program named a.out unless the −o linker option (see below) is used.

Files with .c extensions are treated as C source programs. These programs may be preprocessed, compiled, optimized, assembled link-edited, or have code inserted for profiling. Files with .i extensions are treated as preprocessed C source programs. These may be compiled, optimized, assembled, link-edited, or have code inserted for profiling. Files with .s extensions are treated as assembly source programs. These may be assembled and link-edited.

The compilation process may be stopped after the completion of any compiler pass if the appropriate options are given. If the assembler pass is completed, an object program is produced and left in a file whose name is the same as that of the source program, except that an .o extension is substituted for an .s. If a single C program is compiled and immediately linked, the .o file is ordinarily deleted. Files with extensions other than .c, .s, or .i are passed directly to the linker.

If the cc command is contained in a file with a prefix, *prefix* (i.e., the filename is *prefix*cc), then the prefix will be parsed from the command and used in calling tools. For example, *PROG*cc will call *PROG*acomp, *PROG*basicblk, *PROG*newoptim, *PROG*as, and *PROG*ld, and will link *PROG*crt1.o. Thus, care must be used if the cc command is moved from file to file. The prefix applies to the preprocessor, compiler, optimizer, assembler, link editor, and start-up routines.

The return value from any compiled C program is random unless exit (Peterson 1991a) is called or unless the main() function is left by using a "return construct."

The cc command must be executed in a directory where file creation is permitted, since cc normally creates files in the current directory. However, the cc command does automatically set the mode of executable modules to give permission for execution.

The order in which filenames are specified on the cc command line matters in resolving external references.

Options and Arguments

The options of cc are described below. Any option that cc does not recognize is passed to the loader.

−A *name* [*token*(s)] works like an #assert preprocessing directive. system(unix), cpu(M32), and machine(u3b2) are preassertions.

−A − causes predefined preassertions and predefined macros (except macros that begin with ──) to be forgotten.

−a is passed, with its arguments, directly to the loader. See 1d (CP).

−B{dynamic|static} makes the link editor search for files named libx.so and then for files named libx.a if −B dynamic and −1x are specified. −B static makes the link editor search for files named libx.a. The −B option may be given more than once on the command line as a toggle. cc passes this option and its arguments to 1d (CP).

−C makes the preprocessor phase pass along all comments except those on preprocessor directive lines.

−c suppresses link editing and does not remove object files that may be created.

−Dname[= token(s)] has the same action as a #define in that it associates name with the specified token(s). token is 1 by default if no token is supplied. u3b2 and unix are predefined.

−d{y|n} specifies static linking if −dn is given. Otherwise, the default, −dy, specifies dynamic linking. This option is passed to the linker, together with its arguments.

−E preprocesses the specified C files and sends the result to the standard output. The result will contain preprocessor directives to be used by the next compiler pass.

−e is passed, with any of its arguments, directly to the loader. See 1d (CP).

−f is an obsolete option. The compiler will ignore it.

−F is an obsolete option. The compiler will ignore it.

−G directs the linker to create a shared object instead of a dynamically linked executable. −G is passed to 1d (CP). This option cannot be used with −dn.

−g causes the compiler to generate symbol table information needed by the symbolic debugger, sdb (CP).

−H sends to stderr the pathname of each file included during the present compilation.

−h is passed, with any of its arguments, directly to the loader. See 1d (CP).

−I dir makes cc search in dir for included files whose names do not begin with / instead of starting the search in the usual places.

−J sfm specifies libsfm.sa, the assembly language source math library. libsfm.sa is a special-purpose library that supports in-line expansion of fast, single-precision math functions. The placement of this option on the command line is important because this library is searched when its name is encountered. −O and −Ksd must both be specified in order for this argument to be passed to the optimizer.

−K[mmode, optgoal, PIC, minabi] can take one or more of the following four arguments. If two or more arguments are used with −K, they must be separated by commas, for example, −K fpe, sz. The arguments have the following effects:

mmode causes software floating point emulation if mmode is fpe or specifies use of the hardware math accelerator unit to support floating point calculations if *mmode* is mau.

optgoal establishes the goal of optimization. It causes cc to optimize for speed if *optgoal* is sd or to optimize for size if *optgoal* is sz. −O must be specified in order for *optgoal* to take effect.

PIC causes generation of position-independent code (PIC).

minabi causes the compiler system to use a C library version that minimizes dynamic linking but does not change the ABI conformance or nonconformance of the application. No application that uses the X library or the Network Services library may use −K minabi.

−L *dir* adds *dir* to the list of directories for which *ld* searches. cc passes this option and its arguments to *ld*.

−l *name* searches the library lib*name*.so or the library lib *name*.so. The position of this option on the command line determines when the specified library will be searched relative to other object files and libraries specified on the command line. cc passes this option and its arguemnts to *ld*.

−m is passed directly to the loader. See *ld* (CP).

−O optimizes object code during the compiler phase. The −O option has no effect on .s files. Files with .o extensions are ignored and passed to the linker as is. −O will be ignored if −ql is specified

−o *outfile* produces an output object file named *outfile*. The default *outfile* is a.out. The −o option is passed to *ld*.

−P preprocesses the specified C files, putting the result in corresponding files with .i suffixes. Unlike −E, output caused by −P will not contain any preprocessing directives.

−p causes the compiler to produce code to count the number of times each routine is called. If link editing is specified, monitor (Peterson 1992a) is called and profiled versions of libc.a and libm.a (with the −lm option) are linked if the −dn option is called. If object program execution terminates normally, the file mon.out is produced. It contains execution counts. Thereafter, prof (CP) can produce an execution profile.

−Q{y|n} causes identification information about each invoked compilation tool to be added to the output file if −Qy is specified (the default). Otherwise, if −Qn is specified, identification information is suppressed.

−q{l|p} causes the invocation of the basic block analyzer and causes creation of code that counts the number of times each source line is executed if −ql is specified. lprof can then be used to generate a list of these counts. The −qp option gives results identical to those of −p.

−r is passed directly to the loader. See *ld* (CP).

−S compiles and optimizes (if −O is specified) but does not assemble or link edit the specified C programs and puts assembly language output in corresponding files with .s suffixes.

−s is passed directly to the loader. See ld (CP).

−t is passed directly to the loader. See ld (CP).

−U has the effect of an #undef preprocessor directive. It causes any definition of *name* to be forgotten. If *name* appears in both −D and −U, *name* is not defined, regardless of the order in which the two options appear.

−u is passed directly to the loader. See ld (CP).

−V makes each invoked compilation tool print its version information on stderr.

−v makes cc do more (and stricter) semantic checks and makes cc enable certain *lint* checks.

−W*tool,arg1*[,*arg2* ...] sends arguments *arg1* through *argi* to the specified compilation tool. Each argument must be separated from the preceding argument by a comma. If a backslash (\) precedes a comma, the comma may be used as part of an argument. Values of *tool* specify compilation tools as follows:

0 specifies the compiler.
2 specifies the optimizer.
a specifies the assembler.
b specifies the basic block analyzer.
1 specifies the link editor.
p is a synonym for 0.

For example, −W1,−I *name* makes the linking phase override the default name of the dynamic linker.

−X{a|c|t} specifies the degree of conformance to the ANSI standard. The predefined macro __STDC__ is 0 for −Xa or −Xt and is 1 for −Xc. The effects of the arguments of X are as follows:

−Xt (transition) specifies that the compiled langauge is to include all new ANSI features that are compatible with pre-ANSI C (the default). The compiler warns about any language constructs that differ between ANSI and pre-ANSI C, including the use of trigraphs, changes to integral promotion rules, and the new escape sequence \a.

−Xa (ANSI) specifies inclusion of all new features of ANSI C. Where the interpretation of language constructs differs between ANSI and pre-ANSI C, the ANSI interpretation is used. The compiler warns about integral promotion rules but does not warn about the use of trigraphs or the new escape sequences.

−Xt (conformance) causes the compiled language and associated header files to conform to ANSI and to include all the conforming extensions of −Xa specified above. Only ANSI defined identifiers are visible in the header files.

−Y *item, dirname* specifies a new directory, *dir*, for the location of *item*. *item* may be one of the characters [02ab1p], with the same meaning as in −W above, or it may be one of the following characters representing directories that contain special files:

F is obsolete. Use −YP to simulate the effect of −YF. −YF will be deleted from the next release.

I specifies the directory to be searched last for include files (see INCDIR under "FILES" below).

L is obsolete. Use −YP to simulate the effect of −YL. −YL will be deleted from the next release.

P specifies new default directories to be searched for libraries. *dirname* is a path list with its components separated by colons.

S specifies a directory containing start-up routines: LIBDIR.

U is obsolete. Use −YP to simulate the effect of −YU. −YU will be deleted from the next release.

−z is passed directly to the loader. See 1d (CP).

filenames specifies C source files (*file*.c) or assembler source files (*file*.s) to be compiled.

Files

a.out	link editor output
file.c	C source file
file.i	C source file, preprocessed
file.o	object file
file.s	assembly language file
BINDIR/as	assembler, as
BINDIR/ld	link editor, 1d
BINDIR	ordinarily is /usr/ccs/bin.
INCDIR	ordinarily is /usr/lib/include.
LIBDIR	ordinarily is /usr/ccs/lib.
LIBDIR/acomp	preprocessor and compiler
LIBDIR/basicblk	basic block analyzer
LIBDIR/*crt1.o	start-up routine
LIBDIR/*crti.o	start-up initialization code
LIBDIR/*crtn.o	last start-up routine
LIBDIR/newoptim	optimizer
LIBDIR/libc.so	standard C library, shared
LIBDIR/libc.a	standard C library, archive
LIBDIR/optim	optimizer
TMPDIR/*	temporary files
TMPDIR	ordinarily is /var/tmp; however, it may be redefined by setting the environmental variable TMPDIR [see tmpnam (Peterson 1992a)].

See Also

as (CP), ld (CP), lint (CP), lprof (CP), monitor (Peterson 1991), prof (CP), sdb (CP), tmpnam (Peterson 1992a)
C Compilation System chapter (AT&T 1990a)

cdc (CP)   SOURCE CODE CONTROL SYSTEM   cdc (CP)

Name

cdc—change delta commentary in SCCS s-file(s)

Synopsis

cdc -r*SID* [-m[*mrlist*]] [-y[*comments*]] *filenames*

Description

cdc changes the delta commentary of each SCCS file specified in the cdc command line that has the SID specified in the −r option. The delta commentary is the comment and MR previously specified by the −m and −y arguments of the delta (CP) command.

Permission to change the delta commentary requires permission to make the delta in the first place. Changing the delta commentary requires ownership of both the file and the directory.

Text controlled by SCCS must be interpretable by the standard UNIX editors (ed and vi).

Options and Arguments

The following arguments may appear in any order, and each applies independently to each file named:

−m*mrlist* specifies a list of MR entries to be deleted from the delta commentary of an SCCS s-file if they already exist or to be added if they do not already exist. In order for MR entries to be deleted from and/or added to the delta commentary, the SCCS s-file must have its v flag set [see v in admin (CP)]. The MRs are added to or deleted from the delta commentary of the *SID* specified by the −r keyletter below.

If the v flag has a value assigned, it is treated as the name of a shell procedure or program for validating MR numbers. The cdc command terminates without changing the delta commentary if the validation program returns a nonzero exit status.

A null list of MRs has no effect. The MRs in an MR list must be separated by blanks and/or tab characters. Any newline character ends the MR list unless the newline is preceded by an escape character.

A ! character in front of the MR number of any MR entry indicates that it is to be deleted. The cdc command causes any deleted MRs to be listed in the comment section of the delta commentary, preceded by a comment line saying that the MRs have been deleted. The cdc command adds MR entries to the MR list in the same way that the admin (CP) command does.

The prompt MRs? is sent to the standard output before the standard input is read if the standard input is a terminal and if the −m argument is not used. No prompt is sent if the standard output is not a terminal. The MRs? prompt always occurs before the comments? prompt (see −y).

The −m argument (and the −y argument) must be used if SCCS filenames are given to cdc on the command line (standard input).

−rSID specifies the SID of a delta that is to have its delta commentary changed. The −r argument always specifies an SID in any SCCS command.

−y [comments] gives a new comments string that replaces old comment string(s) for the delta specified by −r. The old comments are retained, preceded by a line announcing that they have been changed. The −y argument (and the −m argument) must be used if SCCS filenames are given to cdc on the command line (standard input). The prompt comments? is sent to standard output before standard input is read if −y is not given and if the standard input is a terminal. No prompt is sent if the standard input is not a terminal. The comments? prompt is always preceded by an MRs? prompt (see the −m option).

Null comments have no effect. A newline character will terminate comments text unless the newline character is preceded by an escape character.

filenames names the SCCS s-file(s) which will have delta commentary changed. If filenames is −, cdc treats each line of the standard input as the name of an SCCS file to be processed. If filename is −, the −m and −k letters must be used. If a directory is specified by filenames, then cdc treats each file in the directory as a file to be processed. However, unreadable files and files lacking a .s prefix are ignored.

Files

See the "FILES" section of the entry for the get (CP) command for a description of all SCCS files.

x-file   See admin (CP), delta (CP), and get (CP).

z-file   See delta (CP), delta (CP), and get (CP).

See Also

admin (CP), comb (CP), delta (CP), get (CP), help (CP), prs (CP), rmdel (CP), sact (CP), sccsdiff (CP), unget (CP), val (CP), vc (CP), what (CP), sccsfile (F)

Name

cflow—make a C flowgraph charting external references

Synopsis

cflow [-r] [-ix] [-i] [-dnum] filenames

Description

After analyzing a collection of files that may be assembler, C, lex, object, and yacc files, cflow gathers information from symbol tables and builds a graph that tells which procedures are called by other procedures. Files that have .s suffixes are assembled. cflow extracts symbol table information from these assembled files, as well as from object files suffixed with .o, for use in building the graph of external references. Files that have .y, .1, or .c suffixes are processed by yacc, lex, or the C compiler, respectively.

cflow prints its output on the standard output. Each line of standard output consists of a reference number, some number of tabs indicating the nesting level, the name of a global symbol, a colon, and the definition of the global symbol. Ordinarily, only those function names that do not begin with an underscore are listed (but see -ix and -i below).

For symbols derived from C source language, the symbol definition consists of a type definition (e.g., int), the name of the source file (delimited by < >), and the line number where the definition was located. Leading underscores (_) in C external names are removed.

Symbol definitions gotten from object files indicate both the filename and the program location counter where the symbol appeared.

If multiple definitions of a symbol occur, cflow issues a warning and believes only the first definition. After the definition of a symbol has been printed, future references to the symbol consist of the reference number of the line where the symbol is defined. Only < > is printed for references that are undefined.

The cflow command can fail to work correctly when it is given files produced by lex (CP) or yacc (CP) because these commands reorder line number declarations. Give cflow (CP) the input to lex or yacc in order to correct this problem.

Options and Arguments

-D has the same action as -D in cc (CP).

-dnum cuts off the graph at the nesting depth specified by num. If the nesting depth is too deep, cflow output can be piped to pr (AT&T 1990q), using the −e option of pr to compress tab expansion to something conveniently less than eight spaces.

−I has the same action as −I in cc (CP).

−i— includes procedures whose names begin with an underscore. The default condition is the exclusion of these functions (data, too, if −ix is specified).

−ix includes external and static data symbols in the graph. Otherwise, only functions are included.

−r generates an inverted listing that shows the callers of each function, sorted in lexicographical order by callee.

−U has the same action as −U in cc (CP).

filenames specifies the files to be processed by cflow. Before being processed by cflow, files with .c, .1, or .y suffixes are processed by cc (CP), lex (CP), and yacc (CP), respectively. The results of this processing, as well as any files with .i suffixes, are next processed by the first pass of lint (CP). Files with .s suffixes are assembled. The cflow command then extracts information from the symbol tables of assembled files and any files with .o suffixes.

See Also

as (CP), cc (CP), lex (CP), lint (CP), nm (CP), yacc (CP), pr (AT&T 1990q)

cof2elf (CP)   OBJECT FILE MANIPULATION   cof2elf (CP)

Name

cof2elf—translate COFF files to ELF files

Synopsis

cof2elf [−iqV] [−Q{y|n}] [−s directory] filename . . .

Description

cof2elf converts COFF file(S) to ELF files. The contents of the actual COFF files are modified.

cof2elf is used in converting to ELF when source code is unavailable. It may be preferable to recompile source code if possible, since cof2elf discards some debugging information. This may affect information used in symbolic debugging.

Options and Arguments

-i causes cof2elf to modify a file even though partial translation conditions such as unknown relocation types exist. These partial translation conditions will otherwise be treated as errors and prevent translation.

-Q*argument* causes identification information about cof2elf to be added to output files if *argument* is y. Otherwise, if *argument* is n, cof2elf adds no identification information to the file(s). The default is for cof2elf not to add identification information.

-q suppresses the message that tells whether a file was translated or saved.

-s*directory* saves a copy of the original COFF file(s) in the specified directory. The directory must exist. If cof2elf does not modify a file, it does not save that file.

-V causes cof2elf to print a version message on the standard error output.

filename specifies the input COFF file(s) to be translated. If an input file is an archive file, each archive member that requires translation will be translated. Afterward, the files in the archive will be in their original order.

Any input file that is not a COFF file will not be translated. Executable or static shared library files are not translated because the operating system supports executable files and static shared libraries (translation is thus unnecessary), and because executable files and static shared libraries have address and alignment constraints that are specific to the file format.

See Also

ld (CP), a.out (F), ar (F), elf (Peterson 1992a)

---

comb (CP)   SOURCE CODE CONTROL SYSTEM   comb (CP)

Name

comb—generate a shell procedure to reconstruct SCCS files

Synopsis

comb -o -s [-p*SID*] [-c*list*] *filenames*

Description

comb creates a shell procedure that reconstructs the specified SCCS files when executed. The purpose is to make reconstructed files that are smaller than the originals, but sometimes the reconstructed file that comb creates may be larger than the original. Also, the shape of the tree of deltas may be rearranged.

Options and Arguments

Keyletter arguments may be specified in any order. If no keyletter arguments are specified, comb preserves leaf deltas and just enough ancestors to preserve the tree. Each keyletter argument applies independently to each SCCS file. If keyletter arguments are specified, they are as follows:

−c*list* instructs comb to preserve deltas in *list*. It causes other deltas to be discarded. See get (CP) for the syntax of *list*.

−o causes the reconstructed file to be accessed at the release of the delta to be created instead of at the most recent ancestor (when a get −e is executed). This option may change the shape of the delta tree of the original file. It may also decrease the size of the reconstructed SCCS file.

−p*SID* specifies the *SID* of the oldest delta that is to be saved. Older deltas are deleted from the reconstructed file.

−s causes comb to create a shell procedure that generates a report for each file, giving the filename, file size (number of blocks) after combination, original size (number of blocks), and percentage change in file size, as computed by

100 * (original size−combined size) / original size

This option should be used to find out how much space will be saved if SCCS files are combined.

filenames specifies the SCCS file(s) to be reconstructed. If a filename of − is specified, each line of the standard input is treated as the name of an SCCS file, except that unreadable files and non-SCCS files are ignored. If a directory is specified as part of *filenames*, each file in the directory is treated as if it had been specified for processing. Again, unreadable files and non-SCCS files are ignored.

FILES

See the "FILES" subsection of the entry for the get (CP) command for a description of all SCCS files.

s.COMB is the reconstructed SCCS file.

comb????? is a temporary file.

See Also

admin (CP), cdc (CP), delta (CP), get (CP), help (CP), prs (CP), rmdel (CP), sact (CP), sccsdiff (CP), unget (CP), val (CP), vc (CP), what (CP), sccsdiff (F), sh (AT&T 1990q)

cscope (CP)   C DEBUGGING AIDS   cscope (CP)

Name

cscope—interactively browse C source code

Synopsis

cscope [-f *reffile*] [-i *namefile*] [[-I *incdir*]] [-d]
[*filenames*]

Description

cscope enables programmers to browse C source code interactively. It builds symbol cross-reference tables the first time it is used to browse a source file. Thereafter, cscope regenerates symbol cross-reference tables for a file only if the contents of the source file(s) or the list of files have changed since the last time cscope was invoked. The command saves time in regenerating symbol tables by copying symbol cross-reference data for unchanged files from the old cross reference to the new.

Unless otherwise specified, cscope builds a symbol cross reference based on examination of the C (.c and .h), lex (.1), and yacc (.y) source files in the current directory. The command uses the cross-reference table to locate references to C function declarations, C function calls, and C preprocessor symbols.

In addition to processing source files that are in the current directory, cscope can process any source files that are specified on the command line. In both cases, cscope searches the standard directories for any #include files that it does not encounter in the cuurrent directory.

cscope is able to recognize function definitions that have the following form:

blank [*return_type*] *functname blanks* (*args*) *white space arg_declars whitespace* {

where

blank is zero or more blanks or tabs, but not newlines, at the start of a line.
[*return_type*] is an optional return type.
functname is the name of the function.
blanks is zero or more spaces or tabs, but not newlines.
args is a string that does not contain either a " or a newline.

cscope fails to recognize some language constructs. In particular, cscope cannot recognize:

- Operator function definitions
- A function declaration inside a function
- A global definition if a preprocessor statement prevents it
- A typedef name preceding a preprocessor statement
- A function definition or call because of braces inside #if statements
- A variable because of braces inside #if statements
- A function that follows another function on a line of code.

Requesting the First Cross-Reference Search

Before asking for the first cross-reference search, set the environment variables below as needed. Their effects are as follows:

EDITOR specifies the editor. The default is vi (AT&T 1990q).

HOME specifies the home directory; it is set at login.

INCLUDEDIRS specifies a colon-separated list of directories to search for #include files.

SHELL specifies the shell. The default is sh (AT&T 1990q).

SOURCEDIRS specifies a colon-separated list of directories to search for additional source files.

TERM specifies the terminal type. It must be a screen terminal.

TERMINFO specifies the full pathname of the terminal information directory. See curses (AT&T 1990h) and terminfo (AT&T 1990h) for instructions for making a terminal description.

TMPDIR specifies the temporary file directory. Its default is /var/tmp.

VIEWER specifies a file display program (e.g., pg) which overrides the EDITOR environment variable.

VPATH gives an ordered list of directory names separated by colons. The cscope command searches for source files in the directories in the list if VPATH is set. Otherwise, cscope searches only the current directory. cscope searches for header files in VPATH if VPATH is set. Otherwise, cscope searches for header files in the the current directory, in directories specified by cscope's −I option, and in the standard directory for header files. Ordinarily, this is /usr/include.

After the cscope command is started, it builds the cross reference and displays the following menu:

```
Find this C symbol:
Edit this function definition:
List functions called by this function:
```

List functions calling this function:
Find this text string:
Change this text string:
Find this grep pattern:
Find this file:
Find files #including this file:

Repeatedly pressing the TAB key moves the cursor to the appropriate input field of the menu. Pressing the RETURN key after typing the text to be searched for activates the first search.

Subsequent Cross-Reference Requests

If the first cross-reference search succeeds, the user can enter any of the single-character commands in the following list. Their effects are as follows:

+ displays the next group of matching lines.

− displays the previous group of matching lines.

1−9 edits the file designated by the line number, 1–9.

> appends the displayed list of lines to the file.

SPACE displays the next group of matching lines.

^e enables editing of displayed files in order.

| pipes all lines to a shell command.

Any of the single-character commands below may be used whenever needed. Their effects are as follows:

TAB moves the cursor to the next input field.

RETURN moves the cursor to the next input field.

? displays this list of commands.

^b moves the cursor to the previous input field and search pattern.

^c toggles use/nonuse of letter case in searches.

^d exits from cscope.

^f moves to the next input field and search pattern.

^l redraws the screen.

^n moves the cursor to the next input field.

^p moves the cursor to the previous input field.

^r rebuilds the cross reference.

^y searches using the last text that was typed.

! starts an interactive shell. Return to cscope by typing ^d.

Substituting New Text for Old

Type the old text which is to be changed. In response, cscope will prompt for the new text that is to be substituted for the old, after which it will display lines containing the old text. The single-character commands below choose the lines to be changed. Their effects are as follows:

! starts an interactive shell. Return to cscope by typing ^d.

* marks or unmarks the displayed lines for change.

+ displays the next group of lines.

− displays the previous group of lines.

1−9 marks or unmarks the lines to be changed.

? gives information about cscope commands in this list.

ESCAPE exits without changing lines marked for change.

SPACE displays the next group of lines.

a marks all of the lines that are to be changed.

^d exits after changing the marked lines.

^1 redraws the screen.

Line-Oriented User Interface

See the −1 option below. If this option is specified, cscope will use >> to prompt for an input line starting with the field number (counting begins at 0) followed by the search pattern. For example, 1main locates the definition of the main function.

cscope outputs the number of reference lines. For each reference it finds, cscope outputs a line that consists of the filename, function name, line number, and line text, separated by spaces.

cscope will quit when it encounters an input line whose first character is ^d or q, or when it encounters an end of file.

Special Keys on the Terminal

If the terminal being used has an arrow key that works in vi (AT&T 1990q), the up-arrow key can be used to move to the previous field instead of using the TAB key repeatedly. Likewise, if the terminal has CLEAR, NEXT, or PREV keys, they can perform the same actions as the ^1, +, and − commands, respectively.

Options and Arguments

−b builds the cross reference only.

−C specifies that letter case is to be ignored in making searches.

−c suppresses data compresssion in the cross-reference file, i.e., only ASCII characters are used in the file.

−d tells cscope not to update the cross reference.

−e suppresses appearance of the ^e prompt between files.

−f *reffile* puts the cross reference in *reffile* instead of in cscope.out (the default file).

−I *incdir* makes cscope search *incdir* for any #include files having names that are not specified in *namefile* or on the command line and that do not begin with / (#include file names can be delimited by " " or < >). First, cscope searches the current directory, then it searches *incdir*. Finally, it searches INCDIR (INCDIR usually is /usr/include). If −I is specified more than once on the command line, the directories are searched in the order of their appearance on the command line. This option can be in the cscope.files file.

−i *namefile* tells cscope to browse the list of files given in *name file* (with filenames separated by newlines, spaces, and tabs), rather than browsing the default source files (cscope.files). cscope ignores any filenames appearing on the command line if −i is specified.

−L is used with the −*num pattern* option below. Together, these two options cause a single search with line-oriented output.

−l allows the use of cscope where a screen-oriented interface would not be useful, for example, from another screen-oriented program. See "Line-Oriented User Interface" above.

−*num pattern* tells cscope to find *pattern*, starting its search at input field *num* (counting from 0).

−P prepends *path* to relative filenames in an existing cross-reference file in order to avoid having to change to the directory where the cross-reference file was built. The −d option must be used with this option.

−p *num* displays the last *num* components of the file path instead of displaying the default (1). If *num* is 0, the filename will not be displayed at all. This option can be in the cscope.files file.

−s *dir* tells cscope to search *dir* for more source files. If no source files are specified on the command line, cscope ignores −s.

−T specifies the use of only the first 8 characters to match C symbols. No regular expression that contains special characters other than a period (.) will match any symbol if its minimum length is longer than 8 characters. This option can be in the cscope.files file.

−U suppresses file stamp checking, thereby assuming that no files have changed.

−u causes cscope to assume that all files have changed. Thus, the cross-reference file is built unconditionally.

−V prints the version number of cscope on the first line of the screen.

filenames specifies the list of files to be browsed. This parameter is ignored if −i *namefile* is specified.

Files

cscope.files are default files that contain the -I, -p, and -T options and the list of source files. See the -i option.

cscope.out is the symbol cross-reference file. It is put in the home directory if it cannot be put in the current directory.

INCDIR is a standard directory for #include files. Ordinarily this directory is /usr/include.

nscope.out is a file that temporarily stores a new cross reference before it replaces an old cross reference.

See Also

cscope chapter (AT&T 1990g)

---

ctrace (CP)   C DEBUGGING AIDS   ctrace (CP)

Name

ctrace—trace execution of a C program

Synopsis

ctrace [options] [file]

Description

ctrace lets the user watch the execution of a C program statement by statement. The effect of ctrace is like that of executing a shell procedure with the -x option.

ctrace inserts statements in the source code of a .c file that print out the text of each executable statement, as well as the value of every variable that is modified or referred to. Finally, ctrace writes the modified .c file to standard output. The output from ctrace has to be put into a temporary file before it can be compiled because cc (CP) cannot use a pipe.

Each program statement is listed at the terminal as it executes. Each statement is followed by the name and the value of any variables that are modified by the statement or to which the statement refers. Any output from the statement follows these values.

ctrace detects loops in trace output and stops tracing until either a new sequence of statements within the loop is executed or the loop is exited. It prints a warning message each 1000 times a loop is executed.

ctrace sends its output to the standard output, where it can be put into a file and examined using bfs (AT&T 1990q), tail (AT&T 1990q), or an editor.

Bugs and Difficulties

ctrace always treats pointers as pointers to character strings. Also, it cannot select a format to print the elements of arrays, structures, and unions when the whole of such an aggregate is assigned rather than an individual element. Thus, ctrace may mistakenly use the wrong format or print the address of an aggregate when the value of an aggregate is required.

ctrace eliminates loop trace output separately for each file of a multifile program. Thus, functions may be called from a loop that is still being traced, or trace output from one function in a file may be eliminated until another function in the same file is called.

Syntax Errors

Here are some syntax errors that will produce ctrace syntax error messages:

- Using functions with the same names as system functions, but with different numbers of arguments;
- Omitting the semicolon just before the right brace (}) at the end of the last element declaration in a structure or union; and
- Using #defined constants (e.g., NULL or EOF) or preprocessor macros as variables.

cc Diagnostic Messages

Code traced by ctrace may cause cc (CP) error messages or warning messages in addition to ctrace messages:

- "compiler takes size of function" means preprocess the ctrace input, using its −P option, as well as any −D, −I, or −U options needed. If messages continue, see the "Syntax Errors" section above for possible syntax errors.
- "out of tree space; simplify expression" means reduce n in the −t n option to less than 10. This reduces the number of traced variables per statement. After reducing n, ignore warnings that ctrace has too many variables to trace.
- "redeclaration of signal" means correct this declaration of signal (Peterson 1991a). Alternatively, remove it and #include <signal.h>.
- "warning: illegal combination of pointer and integer" should be ignored.
- "warning: statement not reached" should be ignored.
- "warning: sizeof returns 0" should be ignored.
- "yacc stack overflow" means that an if . . . else if sequence is too long. Remove an else from the middle.

ctrace Diagnostic Messages
- "cannot handle preprocessor code, use −P option" may be caused by a semi-colon following a #define preprocessor statement or by #ifdef/#endif statements in a C statement, so the code should be preprocessed before it is traced.
- " 'if . . . else if' sequence is too long" means that an if . . . else if sequence is too long. Remove an else from the middle.
- "possible syntax error, try −P option" means use the −P option to preprocess input for ctrace; use any of the −D, −I, or −U options that are appropriate. Also, be sure that BADMAG, EOF, and NULL are not declared as variables.
- "warning: some variables are not traced in this statement" means that n in the −t n option may be set at too low a number. By default, only 10 variables are traced per statement in order to prevent a C compiler "out of tree space; simplify expression" error.
- "warning: statement too long to trace" means that a C statement is more than 400 characters long. Reduce the number of characters by indenting the code with tabs, not spaces.

Options and Arguments

The purpose of each ctrace argument is discussed in the following sections.

Change the Trace Print Function

−p *string* substitutes *string* for 'printf('. See −r *file* for a more far-reaching option.

−r *file* substitutes *file* for the runtime.c trace function package, allowing the whole print function to be changed, not just the name and leading arguments. See −p *string* above.

Choose Functions to Be Traced

By default, ctrace traces all of the program files unless the −f or −v arguments choose a subset of functions to trace. It is also possible to turn tracing on and off and to get statement-by-statement control of tracing by inserting ctron() and ctroff() function calls in a program to turn tracing on and off at run time. Since ctrace defines the preprocessor variable, CTRACE, code involving ctron() and ctroff() can be included conditionally. This permits the use of complex and arbitrary criteria for controlling tracing. For example:

```
#ifdef CTRACE
    if(n=='*' && m<500)
    ctroff();
#endif
```

-f *functions* traces only the specified *functions*.

-v *functions* traces all except the specified *functions*. These two functions can be called from **sdb** (CP) if they are previously compiled using the **-g** option of **sdb**.

Choose Subsets of Lines and Variables to Trace

-l *n* examines *n* consecutively executed statements to get looping trace output, instead of examining 20 statements, the default. Set *n* to 0 to get all trace output from loops.

-s suppresses all redundant trace output from string copy function calls and from simple assignment statements. Use of this option can hide a bug that is caused by using the = operator when a = = is meant to be used.

-t *n* traces *n* variables per statement (20 maximum). The default is 10. Use this option if the compiler says "out of tree space; simplify expression."

Choose Printing Formats

The following default formats are used for printing variables: Double variables are printed in scientific notation as floating point numbers. All long and pointer variables are printed as signed integers. Variables that are of type char, int, or short are sometimes printed as integers, but they may be printed as characters. In addition to these defaults four options may be used to specify formats for printing variables as follows:

-e specifies floating point format.

-o specifies octal format.

-u specifies unsigned format.

-x specifies hexadecimal format.

Preprocess Input Before Tracing

-P runs **cc** to preprocess the input before it is traced.

-D is same as the **-D** option of **cc** (CP).

-I is same as the **-I** option of **cc** (CP).

-U is same as the **-U** option of **cc** (CP).

Get Information About ctrace

-Q*arg* adds identification information about **ctrace** to output files if *arg* is **y**. The default, **n**, asks that no identification information be added to the output file.

-V prints the version number of **ctrace** on the standard error output.

Specify Input File

file holds the C program input to **ctrace**. Input comes from the standard input if *file* is not specified.

Files

/usr/ccs/lib/ctrace/runtime.c contains the run-time trace program.

See Also

sdb (CP), bfs (AT&T 1990p), ctype (Peterson 1992a), fclose (Peterson 1992a), printf (Peterson 1992a), setjmp (Peterson 1992a), signal (Peterson 1991a), string (Peterson 1992a), and tail (AT&T 1990p)

cxref (CP)	C DEBUGGING AIDS	cxref (CP)

Name

cxref—create a cross-reference table for a C program

Synopsis

cxref [options] filenames

Description

cxref builds a cross-reference table for a specified collection of C files. It puts a listing of all symbols (auto, global, static) on standard output for each file or (if the −c option is used) for all files combined. The listing has four fields: NAME, FILE, FUNCTION, and LINE. Line numbers appear in the LINE field. The LINE field also may show reference marks as follows:

= marks an assignment.
− marks a declaration.
* marks a definition.

If the LINE field contains no reference mark, the reference is a general reference.

Symbols in #define statements are processed by cxref, using a special version of cc (CP).

Options and Arguments

−C executes only the first pass of cxref. This creates a .cx file that can later be passed to cxref. Similarly, the −c option of cc causes only the first pass of cc to be performed, and the −c option of lint causes only the first pass of lint to be performed.

−c prints a combined cross-reference table for all input files instead of a separate report for each file on the command line.

−D see the −D option of cc (CP).

−d suppresses printing of declarations in order to make the report more legible.

−F prints the full path of each filename that is referenced.

−I see the −I option of cc (CP).

−l prints global variables and file scope statistics and suppresses printing of local variables.

−Lcols alters the number of columns in LINE (the default is 5 columns).

−o file directs cxref output to file.

−s suppresses the printing of input filenames.

−t specifies the formatting for 80-column listing width.

−U see the −U option of cc (CP).

−V prints the version number of cxref on the standard error output.

−Wname, file, function, line changes the default width of at least one of the fields listed below. The default widths are as follows:

NAME is 15 characters long.
FILE is 13 characters long.
FUNCTION is 15 characters long.
LINE is 20 characters long.

−w <num> specifies that the listing width is num (in decimal). The default width is 80 columns if <num> is not specified or is less than 51.

filenames is a collection of C files to be cross-referenced.

Files

LIBDIR ordinarily is /usr/ccs/lib.

LIBDIR/xref is accessed by cxref.

TMPDIR ordinarily is /var/tmp, however, it can be redefined by altering TMPDIR, the environment variable [see tmpnam (Peterson 1992a).

TMPDIR/cx.* contains temporary files.

TMPDIR/tcx.* contains temporary files.

See Also

cc (CP), lint (CP)

delta (CP)   SOURCE CODE CONTROL SYSTEM   delta (CP)

Name

delta—make a change (delta) to an SCCS file

Synopsis

delta [-r*SID*] [-s] [-n] [-g*list*] [-m[*mrlist*]] [-y[*comment*]] [-p]*filenames*

Description

delta takes changes that were made to an SCCS g-file retrieved by get -e (CP) and puts them in an SCCS s-file, making the changes permanent. delta makes a delta to each specified file. See *filenames* below.

If a get generates a large amount of data, execute get and delta repeatedly instead of executing one get of many files, followed by a delta of those files.

The SOH ASCII (start of heading) character (binary 001) has a special meaning for SCCS when it appears at the beginning of a line, so lines that start with the SOH character must be escaped if they are put in the SCCS file. See sccsfile (F) for details.

Diagnostic Messages

Error messages produced when delta aborts are of the form

ERROR *filename*: *message* (*code*)

Execute help *code* to get an explanation of the error code.

Options and Arguments

Each keyletter argument applies independently to each SCCS file.

-g *list* gives a list of deltas to be ignored when the SCCS file is accessed at the delta level specified for this delta.

-n causes the edited g-file to be retained at the end of delta processing.

-m[*mrlist*] specifies the list of MR numbers given as the reason for this delta. The MR list consists of MR numbers separated by blanks and/or tabs. Any unescaped newline character terminates an MR list. If the v flag in the SCCS file is set (by the admin command), an MR number must be supplied as the reason for creating a new delta. If the v flag has a value, it is treated as the name of a shell procedure or program that validates MR numbers. The delta command terminates if the validation procedure returns a nonzero exit status, because delta assumes that at least one MR was invalid. The prompt MRs? is sent to the standard output if the standard output is a terminal and the −m keyletter is not used. The MRs? prompt that is caused by the absence of −m always precedes the comments? comment that is caused by the absence of the −y keyletter, except that no prompt is sent if the standard output is not a terminal.

−p prints on standard output in diff (AT&T 1990q) format the changes (differences) in an SCCS file caused by a delta.

−rSID specifies which delta is to be made to an SCCS file. This option needs to be used only if the same login name has more than one get −e operation outstanding on the same SCCS file. SID can be the SID given on the get command line or the SID to be created as reported by get (CP). If SID is omitted or is ambiguous, it is an error.

−s prevents listing (on the standard output) of the newly created delta's SID, and the number of lines deleted, inserted, and unchanged.

−y[comment] is an arbitrary string (possibly null) describing the reason for a making a delta. Any newline not preceded by an escape terminates the comment. If the standard input is a terminal and −y is not specified, delta issues a prompt, comments?, on the standard output. Comments can be text strings of at most 1024 characters. If a line length exceeds 1000 characters, it causes undefined results.

filenames specifies the SCCS files to be used as input. If filenames is −, each line of the standard input is treated as the name of an SCCS file to be processed by delta. If the standard input (−) is specified, the −y option (and −m if necessary) must be used. Otherwise, an error occurs. If a directory is specified, delta processes each file in the directory; however, delta ignores unreadable files and non-SCCS files (files lacking .s prefixes).

Files

See admin (CP) and get (CP) for additional details about the following files:

d-file is a temporary copy of the g-file. It is created during delta execution and deleted afterward.

g-file contains changes to be made to an original s-file. It exists before delta execution and is gone after delta execution is completed.

p-file contains the SID of the file being updated, the next SID when the g-file is restored to the s-file, and the login of the user retrieving the g-file. It exists before delta execution and may remain afterward.

q-file is used by delta when it is updating a p-file. It is created during delta execution and deleted afterward.

s-file is the primary SCCS file, holding the original file and deltas to it.
/usr/bin/bdiff computes the differences between *g-file* and the gotten file.

x-file is created whenever changes are made to an s-file. All actual changes are made to the x-file, holding the s-file safe in case of a crash. When changes are complete, the existing s-file is replaced by the x-file.

z-file is a lock file created to prevent simultaneous s-file updates by different users. It contains the process ID of the currently executing SCCS process.

See Also

admin (CP), cdc (CP), comb (CP), get (CP), help (CP), prs (CP), rmdel (CP), sact (CP), sccsdiff (CP), unget (CP), val (CP), vc (CP), what (CP), bdiff (AT&T 1990q), sccsfile (F)

dis (CP)	ASSEMBLY/DISASSEMBLY	dis (CP)

Name

dis—disassemble object code

Synopsis

dis [-o] [-V] [-L] [-s] [-d *sec*] [-D *sec*] [-F *function*] [-t *sec*] [-l *string*] *filename* . . .

Description

dis disassembles an object file or archive file, producing an assembly language listing. The listing consists of assembly statements and the hexadecimal or octal code that gave rise to the statements.

A number enclosed in brackets at the start of an output line (e.g., [6]) indicates that the breakpoint line number begins with the following line. These bracketed line numbers can be produced only if the compiler option -g was used in producing the object file.

Any function name will be displayed in the first column of the output line, followed by ( ) if the object file has a symbol table. For control transfer instructions, the computed address within the section to which control is transferred is given by an expression like <60> in the operand field of the instruction or in the symbolic disassembly.

Options and Arguments

The following keyletter arguments can be specified in any order:

−d *sec* limits disassembly to the specified section, *sec*, and prints the offset of the data from the beginning of *sec*.

−D *sec* limits disassembly to the specified section, *sec*, and prints the actual address of the data.

−F *function* limits disassembly to the specified *function* in each object file given on the command line. This option may be specified more than once.

−L finds source labels in the symbolic table for later printing. The file must have been compiled with the −g option of cc (CP) for the −L option to work.

−l *string* limits disassembly to the archive file named *string*. For example, *string* would be "z" for disassembling libz.a.

−o prints output in octal (default: hexadecimal).

−s causes symbolic disassembly, giving source symbol names for operands when possible. To give maximum symbolic disassembly, the file must be compiled with the −g option of cc (CP).

−t *sec* limits disassembly to the specified section, *sec*, and treats *sec* as text, not data.

−V prints (on standard error) the version number of the disassembler being executed.

filename . . . specifies the object files or archive files to be disassembled.

Files

LIBDIR ordinarily is /usr/ccs/lib. All libraries are assumed to be in LIBDIR.

See Also

as (CP), cc (CP), ld (CP), a.out (F)

---

dump (CP)   **OBJECT FILE MANIPULATION**   **dump (CP)**

Name

dump—dump selected pieces of an object file

Synopsis

dump [*options*] *files*

Description

dump dumps parts of the given *files*, as specified by the options below. Both object files and archives of object files may be dumped. dump chooses character, decimal, octal, or hex formatting for output as appropriate.

Options and Arguments

The dump command has the options and modifiers listed below.

Options

Blanks may be used to separate any option from its modifier.

−a dumps the archive header of each member of the archive.

−C dumps decoded C + + symbol table names.

−c dumps string table(s).

−D dumps debugging information.

−f dumps *files* headers.

−g dumps the global symbols in the archive symbol table.

−h dumps section headers.

−L dumps static shared library information and dynamic linking information.

−l dumps line number information.

−o dumps optional program execution headers.

−r dumps relocation information.

−s dumps the contents of sections in hexadecimal.

−T *indx* dumps the indexed symbol table entry specified by *indx*.

−T *indx1*, *indx2* dumps a range of entries specified by *indx1*, *indx2*.

−t dumps symbol table entries.

−u controls the amount of translation that occurs in translating COFF object files to ELF internally. File contents of the COFF file being read are not affected by this translation. If −u is not specified, COFF values are preserved to the extent possible, and the actual bytes in the file are shown. Otherwise, dump updates the COFF values and does the internal translation. The bytes displayed when −u is used may not match the file itself; they show what the COFF file would look like if it were converted to ELF.

Modifiers

The following modifiers can modify the effects of the above options:

−d *number* or −d *number1*, *number2* dumps sections specified by *number* or dumps the range of sections from *number1* to *number2*, inclusive. −d can be used with the following options: −h, −s, or −r. The −d modifier specifies a range of sections or a section if −d is used with either the

−h or the −s option. If −d is used with the −r option, it specifies a range of sections or a section to which the relocation applies. For example, to print out a specified relocation section, execute dump −sv −n *name* to get interpreted output, or dump −s −n *name* to get raw output. To print out all of the relocation entries associated with a .text section when the .text section is number 2 in the file, execute dump −r −d 2.

−n *name* dumps information for *name* only. −n *name* may be used with options −h, −r, −s, or −t. The −n *name* modifier specifies the name of a section when it is used with −h or −s. If −n is used with −t or −r, *name* specifies a symbol. For example, to dump the symbol table entry for the .text symbol, execute dump −t −n .text. To dump the section header information for the .text section, execute dump −h −n .text.

−p prevents the printing of header information.

−v causes the dump to be in symbolic rather than numeric representation (e.g., C__SHARP rather than 0x04).

The −v modifier may be used with any of the following options in dumping the types of variables given:

−a is used in dumping date, user ID, and group ID variables.

−f is used in dumping class, data, type, machine, version, and flags variables.

−h is used in dumping type and flags variables.

−L is used in dumping value variables.

−o is used in dumping type and flags variables.

−r is used in dumping name and type variables.

−s specifies that section contents such as the string table or symbol table are to be interpreted where possible. For example, dump −s −n .symtab *filenames* prints raw data in hexadecimal format, while dump −sv −n .symtab *filenames* gives the same formatted output as dump −tv *filenames*.

−t is used in dumping type and bind variables.

See Also

a.out (F) ar (F)

---

get (CP)   SOURCE CODE CONTROL SYSTEM   get (CP)

Name

get—generate ASCII text from an SCCS file

Synopsis

get [-rSID] [-ccutoff] [-ilist] [-xlist] [-wstring]
[asequence] [-k] [-e] [-l[p]] [-p] [-m] [-n] [-s] [-b] [-g] [-t]
filename . . .

Description

get creates an SCCS g-file (an ASCII text file) from each specified SCCS
s-file. The name of each output g-file is derived by removing the beginning s
from the corresponding input s-file name. For each file it processes, get reports
(on standard output) the SID being processed and the number of lines that it
retrieved from the SCCS s-file.

Identification Keywords

Identification information can be put into text retrieved from an SCCS file
by substituting the values of identification keywords for the identification keywords themselves, which are described in Table 1-1. The %E% and %U% identification words described in the table can be used for nested gets. The keywords
may be used in text that is stored in an SCCS file.

Table 1-2 shows the allowable SCCS identification strings.

Options and Arguments

The arguments may be specified in any order. Each argument applies independently to each specified SCCS file.

−asequence specifies the delta sequence number of the SCCS file delta
to be retrieved. See sccsfile (F), for additional details. The −a keyletter
is used by the comb (CP) command. If -a is used together with −e, it may
create an unexpected SID. Only −a is used if both −a and −r are specified.
The −r keyletter and the −a and −e keyletters can be used to control naming
of the SID of the impending delta.

−b is used with the −e keyletter to specify that the new delta is to have an
SID in a new branch (see Table 1-2 above). In order for this option to work,
a b flag must be present in the s-file or the retrieved delta must be a leaf delta,
i.e., a delta with no successors in the file tree.

A branch delta can always be created from a nonleaf delta. Partial deltas are
interpreted as shown in Table 1-2 above.

−ccutoff specifies that no deltas applied after the cutoff date are to be

TABLE 1-1.   Identification Keywords

Keyword	Value
`^A^`	Notation for creating `what` strings for non-UNIX system program files; `%A% = %Z%%Y% %M% %I%%Z%`
`%B%`	Delta branch number
`%C%`	Current line number; used for identifying messages that are output by the program, not for providing sequence numbers for every line
`%D%`	Current date (YY/MM/DD)
`%E%`	Creation date of newest applied delta (YY/MM/DD)
`%F%`	SCCS file name
`%G%`	Creation date of newest applied delta (MM/DD/YY)
`%H%`	Current date (MM/DD/YY)
`%I%`	*SID* (`%R%.%L%.%B%.%S%`) of retrieved text
`%L%`	Delta level number
`%M%`	Module name (either the name of the SCCS file with **s** removed if the **m** flag is absent from the file or, if the **m** flag is present, the value of the **m** flag)
`%P%`	SCCS file name (fully qualified).
`%Q%`	Value of a **q** flag in the SCCS file; see `admin`
`%R%`	Delta release number
`%S%`	Delta sequence number
`%T%`	Current time (*HH:MM:SS*)
`%U%`	Creation time of newest applied delta (*HH:MM:SS*)
`%W%`	Notation for creating `what` strings for UNIX system program files. `%W% = %Z%%M%<horizontal-tab>%I%`
`%Y%`	Module type (value of the **t** flag in the SCCS file); see `admin`
`%Z%`	`@(#)`, a 4-character string recognized by `what`

included in the g-file (an ASCII text file described in the "FILES" section below). The format of *cutoff* is *YY*[*MM*[*DD*[*HH*[*MM*[*SS*]]]]]. Any time or date units omitted from the cutoff specification default to their maximum value. For example, `-c9006` defaults to `-c900628235959`. The individual two-digit parts of the cutoff date-time may be separated by any number of nonnumeric characters. This lets the user give a cutoff date in the following form: `-c90/06/01 12:00:00`.

`-e` specifies that the new g-file to be created is to be editable. It causes a p-file to be created. Using the `-e` keyletter in a `get` for a given *SID* prevents additional `get`s for the same *SID* until the `delta` commmand is executed or unless the SCCS file gotten had a **j** (joint editing allowed) flag set by the `admin` (CP) command. It is always possible for SCCS files with different *SID*s to be edited concurrently.

If the g-file created by using `get -e` is accidentally harmed during editing,

TABLE 1-2.   SCCS identification strings

	Results		Initial Conditions	
SID of Retrieved Delta	SID of Impending Delta		SID Specified[1]	Other Initial Conditions[2]
mR.mL	mR.(mL + 1)		None[3]	−b. R defaults to mR.
mR.mL	mR.mL.(mB + 1).1		None[3]	no −b. R defaults to mR.
mR.mL	R.1[4]		R	no −b. R > mR
mR.mL	mR.(mL + 1)		R	no −b. R = mR
mR.mL	mR.mL.(mB + 1).1		R	−b. R > mR
mR.mL	mR.mL.(mB + 1).1		R	−b. R = mR
hR.mL[5]	hR.mL.(mB + 1).1		R	n/r; R<mR; R nonexistent
R.mL	R.mL.(mB + 1).1		R	n/r;[6]
R.L	R.(L + 1)		R.L	no -b.[7]
R.L	R.L.(mB + 1).1		R.L	−b[7]
R.L	R.L.(mB + 1).1		R.L	n/r[8]
R.L.B.mS	R.L.B.(mS + 1)		R.L.B	no −b.[9]
R.L.B.mS	R.L.(mB + 1).1		R.L.B	−b.[9]
R.L.B.S	R.L.B.(S + 1)		R.L.B.S	no −b.[9]
R.L.B.S	R.L.(mB + 1).1		R.L.B.S	−b.[9]
R.L.B.S	R.L.(mB + 1).1		R.L.B.S	n/r. Branch successor

Copyright © 1990 UNIX System Laboratories, Inc. All Rights Reserved. Reprinted with permission.

[1]R, L, B, and S specify the release, level, branch, and sequence parts of the SID, respectively, and m preceding such a part specifier stands for the maximum for that part. For example, "R.L.B.mS" means the maximum sequence number within release R, level L, and branch B. If any part R, L, B, or S of the SID is specified, then that part must exist.

[2]The −b option has an effect only if the b flag is present in the SCCS file. See admin for details. A table entry with "n/r" means that the −b option is irrelevant.

[3]No SID is specified if the d flag (default) is absent from the SCCS file. If d is present, however, the SID gotten from the d flag is treated as if it were specified on the command line.

[4]R.1 forces generation of the first delta in a new release.

[5]hR.mL is the highest release that exists and is lower than the specified nonexistent release R.

[6]The trunk successor in the release is greater than R, and R exists.

[7]There is no trunk successor.

[8]The trunk successor in release is greater than or equal to R.

[9]There is no branch successor.

get −k can re-create it. Using the −e keyletter implies using the −k keyletter below.

The protection for SCCS files that is specified through the use of ceiling, floor, and a list of authorized users is in force when the −e keyletter is used.

The −e keyletter causes the SID of the impending delta to appear after the SID accessed but before the number of lines generated. If more than one file or directory is specified or if the standard input is specified, then before each file is processed, its filename is printed, preceded by a newline.

−g prevents actual retrieval of text from the SCCS file. This is used to verify the existence of a given *SID* or to create an l-file.

−i*list* specifies a *list* of new deltas to be included in the new g-file (see the "FILES" section below). The *list* has the following syntax:

$$<list> ::= <range> \mid <list> , <range>$$
$$<range> ::= SID \mid SID - SID$$

where *SID* may have the form shown in Table 1-2.

The −i option causes included deltas to be listed after the word "included."

−k prevents each identification keyword in the g-file from being expanded to its value. Using −k implies using −e.

−l[p] causes an l-file (the delta summary) not to be created. If lp is specified, no l-file is created. Instead, the delta summary is written to standard output. See the "FILES" section below.

−m precedes each line of text retrieved from the SCCS file by the *SID* of the delta that put the text in the SCCS file and a tab. The format of a line is the *SID*, followed by a horizontal tab, followed by text.

−n causes each generated text line to be preceded by the %M% identification keyword and a tab. If both −m and −n are used, the text line has the following format: %M% value, followed by a tab, followed by the format generated by −m.

−p writes the retrieved text to standard output without creating a g-file. Output normally sent to the standard output is sent to file descriptor 2 instead, unless it is thrown away by specifying the −s keyletter.

−r*SID* uses *SID* to specify the version (delta) of the s-file to be retrieved by get. Table 1-2 above shows how *SID* specifies the version of the SCCS file retrieved. It also shows the *SID* of the version that will later be created by delta (CP) if the −e keyletter is used.

−s prevents output to standard output but not output to standard error (file descriptor 2).

−t accesses the most recently created delta in a specified release or release and level.

−w *string* replaces every occurrence of %W% with *string* when the file is gotten. Substitution is done before keywords are expanded.

−x*list* specifies a *list* of deltas to be excluded from the new g-file. Excluded deltas are listed after the word "excluded." See −i above for the *list* format.

filename . . . specifies SCCS s-files input to get. If a directory is specified, get processes each file in the directory, except that non-SCCS files (the last part of the pathname does not begin with s) and unreadable files are ignored. If – specifies the filenames, each line from the standard input is taken to be the name of an SCCS file to be processed. Non-SCCS files and unreadable files are ignored in this case too.

Files

The get (CP) command creates some auxiliary files, described below. The letter appended before the hyphen is the file tag for these files. The name of each auxiliary file is formed by replacing the leading s of an s-file name by the appropriate file tag, except that the g-file name is derived simply by removing the s prefix. For example, with s-file, s.tuv.c, the g-file is tuv.c, while the l-file, p-file, and z-file are l.tuv.c, p.tuv.c, and z.tuv.c, respectively.

bdiff is a program for computing the differences between the gotten file and the g-file.

d-file is a temporary copy of the g-file, created during delta execution and deleted afterward.

g-file contains changes to be made to an original s-file. It exists before delta execution and is gone after delta execution is completed. The g-file is created whether or not the get generated any lines of text. It is created in the current directory if the –p keyletter is not used. The g-file is owned by the real user. Only the real user needs write permission in the current directory. The mode of the g-file is 644 if the –k option is implied or used; otherwise, the mode is 444.

l-file has a table that tells which deltas were applied in creating the text retrieved by get. If the –l keyletter is used, the l-file is created in the current directory. The mode of the l-file is 444. The l-file is owned by the user; only the real user needs write permission in the current directory. The format of the first few lines in the l-file table is shown in Table 1-3. Comments and MR numbers follow on additional lines, each indented one horizontal character. Each entry is terminated by a blank line.

p-file is used to pass information from a get –e to a delta. The file contains the *SID* of the file being updated, the next *SID* when the g-file is restored to the s-file, and the *login* of the user retrieving the g-file. It exists before delta execution and may remain afterward. The p-file contents prevent any additional executions of get –e until either j, the joint edit flag, is set in the SCCS file or delta is executed. See admin (CP) for additional details. The p-file has the following format:

- The *SID* of the gotten file,
- A blank,

TABLE 1-3.   L-file table format

Line	Format
1.	An * if delta was not applied; otherwise, a blank
2.	Blank if delta was applied or if it was not applied and was ignored, otherwise * if delta was not applied and not ignored
3.	Reason that delta was or was not applied: ''C'' means cutoff (keyletter −c), ''I'' means included, ''X'' means excluded
4.	Blank
5.	SID
6.	Tab character
7.	Date and time of creation (YY/MM/DD HH:MM:SS)
8.	Blank
9.	Login name of delta creator

- The *SID* of the impending delta,
- A blank,
- The login name of the real user,
- A blank,
- The date and time `get` was executed,
- A blank,
- The −i keyletter (if it was present), and
- A newline.

There can be several lines in the p-file at once, but no two lines may have the same *SID* for an impending delta. The p-file is created in the same directory that contains the SCCS file. The effective user must have write permission in the directory. The mode of the directory is 644; it is owned by the effective user.

q-file is used by `delta` when it is updating a p-file. It is created during `delta` execution and deleted afterward.

`/usr/bin/bdiff` is a program to compute the differences between *g-file* and the gotten file.

x-file is created whenever changes are made to an s-file. All actual changes are made to the x-file, holding the s-file safe in case of a crash. When changes are complete, the existing s-file is replaced by the x-file.

z-file is a lock file created to prevent simultaneous s-file updates by different users. It contains the binary process ID (2 bytes) of the SCCS process , i.e., the `get` that created it. The z-file is generated in the directory that contains the SCCS file during the `get`. The z-file has permission mode 444. The protection restrictions that apply to the p-file also apply to the z-file.

See Also

admin (CP), bdiff (AT&T 1990q), cdc (CP), comb (CP), delta (CP), get (CP), help (CP), prs (CP), rmdel (CP), sact (CP), sccsdiff (CP), unget (CP), val (CP), vc (CP), what (CP)

help (CP)   SOURCE CODE CONTROL SYSTEM   help (CP)

Name

help—get help about SCCS commands

Synopsis

help [*arg-type1* or *arg-type2* or *arg-type3*]

Description

help gets information that explains the use of an SCCS command or the message displayed by a command. Type help stuck for information if you are stuck.

Options and Arguments

The help command will prompt for arguments if none is given. If an argument is given, it must be a message number (these normally appear in parentheses after messages) or a command name. The argument may be one of the following types:

arg-type1 is all numeric.

arg-type2 contains no numerics (only command names such as delta).

arg-type3 starts with nonnumerics but ends with numerics. The non-numeric prefix is an abbreviation for the command that generated the message. The numeric suffix designates one of a series of messages that may be produced by a particular SCCS command. For example, ge4 means message 4 from the get command.

Files

See the "FILES" section of the entry for the get (CP) command for a description of all SCCS files.

LIBDIR ordinarily is /usr/ccs/lib.

LIBDIR/help contains files of message text.

LIBDIR/help/helploc is a file that contains locations of help files that are not in LIBDIR/help.

See Also

admin (CP), cdc (CP), comb (CP), delta (CP), get (CP), prs (CP), rmdel (CP), sact (CP), sccsdiff (CP), unget (CP), val (CP), vc (CP), what (CP)

---

install (CP)   SOFTWARE VERSION CONTROL   install (CP)

Name

install—install commands in the file system

Synopsis

/usr/sbn/install [-c *dira*] [-f *dirb*] [-g *group*] [-i] [-m *mode*] [-n *dirc*] [-o] [-s] [-u *usr*] *filename* [*diri* . . .]

Description

install is commonly used in makefiles to install an updated target file, *filename*, in a specified location in a file system. The mode and owner of the original command are retained.

install tells the user which files it is replacing or creating and tells where it is putting these files.

Options and Arguments

-c *dira* installs the new command, *filename*, in the directory specified by *dira* if the command is not already in *dira*. Otherwise, install says that the file already exists, and it exits without overwriting the existing file. -c *dira* may be used alone or with the -s option below.

-f *dirb* installs the new command, *filename*, in directory *dirb* even if *filename* already is in *dirb*. If the *filename* already is in *dirb*, the mode and owner of the new *filename* will be that of the old *filename*. If the *filename* being installed is not already in *dirb*, install sets its mode and owner to 755 and bin, respectively. -f *dirb* may be used alone or with the -o or -s options.

-g *group* sets the group ID of the new command, *filename*, to *group*. This option is available only to the superuser.

−i causes only the directories specified by *dirx* to be searched, not the default directory list. −i may be used alone or with any other options except −c and −f.

−m *mode* sets the mode of the new command, *filename*, to *mode*.

−n *dirc* puts the new command, *filename*, in the directory specified by *dirc* if *filename* is not found in any of the directories searched. install sets the mode and owner to 755 and bin, respectively. −n *dirc* may be used alone or with any other options except −c and −f.

−o saves an existing version of *filename* (if it was found) by copying it to old*filename* in the directory where it was found. This option is for use in installing a frequently used file when the existing file cannot be removed, for example, /usr/bin/sh. This option may be used either alone or with any other options except −c.

−s suppresses printing of all messages except error messages. −s may be used alone or with any other options.

−u *user* sets the owner of the new command, *filename*, to *user*.

dirx specifies the directories which install is to search after it searches the default directories. If no directories *dirx* . . . are specified, install searches the default directories /usr/usr/bin/, /usr/usr/usr/bin, /etc, /usr/usr/lib, and /usr/usr/usr/lib for *filename*. If install finds *filename* it overwrites it and tells the user it is doing so. If install does not find *filename*, it tells the user and exits without taking further action.

filename specifies the command to be installed.

See Also

make (CP)

ld (CP)	**LINK EDITING**	ld (CP)

Name

ld—link-edit common object files

Synopsis

ld [options] *filename* . . .

Description

ld relocates code, resolves external references, and supports symbol tables for symbolic debugging.

In static mode (see −dn below), ld combines relocatable object files (*filename*), in the specified order, into an executable object file. If the −r option (see below) is specified in static mode, relocatable object files are combined to create a relocatable object file.

In dynamic mode (the default mode; see −dy below), ld combines the relocatable files specified in its arguments to create an executable object file that will be linked at run time with any shared object files that are given as arguments. A shared object file is a single entity which has all of its references resolvable within the executable that ld is creating, or resolvable within other shared objects with which it is being linked.

In both static and dynamic mode, ld sends its output to a.out by default.

If an argument specifies a library, ld searches the library only once, at the point it encounters the library in the argument list. However, the ordering of library arguments is unimportant unless there is more than one library member that defines the same external symbol, because ld searches the library archive symbol table ar (AT&T 1990m)] sequentially with as many passes as are required to resolve all of the external references that the library can satisfy. The library can be a relocatable archive or a shared library. ld saves space by loading only those routines that resolve external references.

Options and Arguments

−a generates (in static mode only) an executable object file, the default option for static mode. The −a option cannot be used with the −r option.

−B{dynamic|static} causes shared objects not to be included in the library (if −Bstatic is specified) until a −Bdynamic is encountered on the command line. −Bdynamic is valid only in dynamic mode. These two options, dynamic and static, may be specified on the command line as often as required. They act as a toggle. See the −l option.

−B*symbolic* binds references to global symbols to their definitions within an object (if the definitions are available) in dynamic mode when ld is building a shared object. Even if definitions are available, references to global symbols ordinarily are not bound to their definitions until run time. Thus definitions of a symbol in some object can override the object's definition. If there are any undefined symbols, ld will issue a warning unless the warning is overridden by the −z defs option.

−b suppresses (only when a shared object is being created in dynamic mode) special processing for relocations that refer to symbols in shared objects. Unless −b is specified, the link editor will create special relocations for references to functions defined in shared objects. These references will be independent of position, and ld will cause the dynamic linker to copy data objects that are defined in shared objects into the memory image of the executable at run time.

The −b option will make output code less sharable, though it may make the code more efficient.

−d{y|n} causes ld to use static linking when −dn is specified. Otherwise, −dy, the default, causes ld to use dynamic loading.

−e *esym* makes the address of *esym* the entry point for the output file.

−G combines relocatable object files to create a shared object in dynamic mode only. Undefined symbols are permitted.

−h *name* records *name* in an object's dynamic section if the object is being built in dynamic mode. Instead of the object's UNIX System file name being recorded in executables that are linked with this object, *name* is recorded. Thus, the dynamic linker will seek a shared object called *name* at run time.

−I *name* writes *name* into the program header as the pathname of the interpreter when building an executable. The default name of the interpreter is the name of the dynamic linker, /usr/lib/libc.so.1, when the executable is being built in the dynamic mode. The default in the static mode is that there will be no interpreter. −I overrides either of these default conditions. If −I is used, exec loads the interpreter when it loads the a.out file and it passes control to the interpreter instead of passing it to the interpreter directly.

−L *dir* specifies *dir* as a library to be searched before the standard libraries are searched. −L *dir* must precede −l in order to be effective.

LD_RUN_PATH, an environment variable, contains a directory list that can specify library search directories to the dynamic linker. If LD_RUN _PATH is present but not null, ld passes LD_RUN_PATH to the linker by way of data stored in the output object file.

LD_LIBRARY_PATH, an environment variable, can specify library search directories. Usually LD_LIBRARY_PATH will hold two directory lists separated by a semicolon:

$$dir1;dir2$$

If −L is specified more than once when ld is called, directories are searched in the following order:

$$dir1\ path1\ .\ .\ .\ pathn\ dir2\ \text{LIBPATH}$$

If LD_LIBRARY_PATH exists in the environment, it can specify library search directories to the dynamic linker at run time. If LD_LIBRARY_PATH exists, the dynamic linker will search directories specified by LD_LIBRARY _PATH before it searches its default directory for shared objects that are to be linked with the program at run time.

−l*x* searches a library for shared objects, lib*x*.so, or an archive library, lib*x*.a. If the mode is dynamic and −Bdynamic is specified, ld searches for a file, libx.so or libx.a, in each directory that is given in a library search path. The search ends at the first directory that contains either file. If −lx expands to two files with names of the form libx.so or libx.a, ld will select the file whose name ends in .so. ld will accept libx.a if it cannot find libx.so. If the mode is static or Bstatic is specified, ld will choose only the file whose name ends in .a. The placement of −l in the ld command line matters because ld searches a directory when it encounters the directory name.

−M *mapfile* treats *mapfile* as a text file of directives to ld (in static mode only). Avoid using this option because these directives change the shape of the output file that ld creates.

−m generates a listing or memory map of the I/O section on standard output.

−o *outfile* generates an output object file, *outfile*. The default *outfile* is a.out.

−Q{y|n} adds an *ident* string to the comment section of the output file if −Qy is specified. This identifies the version of ld used to create the file. If there are multiple linking steps, as when using −ld −r, use of −Qy results in multiple ld idents.

−r produces one relocatable object file by combining relocatable object files. −r cannot be used with the −a option, nor can it be used in dynamic mode. ld does not warn about unresolved references if −r is used.

−s strips debug and line sections and their associated relocation entries from *outfile*, the output object file. Also, except for shared objects or relocatable files, ld removes string table and symbol table sections from the output object file.

−t suppresses warnings about multiply defined symbols that have different sizes.

−u *symname* enters *symname* in the symbol table as an undefined symbol. This makes it easy to load routines entirely from an archive library, because it supplies an unresolved reference needed to force loading of the first library routine. The −u *symname* option must be placed on the ld command line before the library that defines the symbol.

−V reports what version of ld is in use.

−YP,*dir* changes the default directory for libraries. The path list, *dir*, is colon separated.

−z *defs* causes a fatal error if any undefined symbols are left when the link is finished. The default is to force an error if if undefined symbols remain. Use of −z defs ensures that any shared object being built will be self-contained, i.e., all of its symbolic references will be resolved internally.

−z *nodefs* permits undefined symbols, the default condition when shared objects are being built. When an executable is being built in dynamic mode, this option permits linking of a shared object that has unresolved references in routines that are not used by the executable.

-z text causes a fatal error (in dynamic mode only) if there remain any relocations against nonwritable, allocatable sections.

filename specifies a relocatable object file to be processed by ld.

Files

a.out is the output file.
libx.a contains libraries.
LIBPATH ordinarily is /usr/ccs/lib:/usr/lib.
libx.so contains libraries.

See Also

as (CP), cc (CP), mkshlib (CP), a.out (F), ar (F), end (Peterson 1992a), exit (Peterson 1991a)

C Compilation System chapter (AT&T 1990a), Mapfile Option appendix (AT&T 1990a)

---

ldd (CP)   **LIBRARY MANAGEMENT**   **ldd (CP)**

Name

ldd—list the dynamic dependencies of a file

Synopsis

ldd [-d|-r] filename

Description

ldd lists the pathnames of all shared objects that will be loaded if file name is executed. ldd will succeed, but without producing output, if filename is an executable file that does not require shared objects.

ldd prints its report of shared object pathnames to standard output stdout. ldd does not report those shared objects that are explicitly attached by using dlopen (Peterson 1992a).

ldd finds shared objects by using the same search algorithm as the dynamic linker.

ldd optionally will print warnings for any unresolved symbol references that will occur if *filename* is executed. These warnings are printed to standard error stderr. Thus, ldd can be used to check the compatibility of *filename* with the shared objects it uses. The options listed in the following section control this use of ldd.

Options

Only one of the following options may be used during each invocation of *ldd*:

−d causes ldd to examine each reference to data objects.

−r causes ldd to examine each reference to data objects or functions.

filename is the file whose requirements for shared objects are to be determined by ldd. If *filename* is not an executable file or if it cannot be opened for reading, ldd returns a nonzero exit status.

See Also

cc (CP), ld (CP)

C Compilation System chapter (AT&T 1990g)

lex (CP)   LEXICAL/SYNTACTICAL ANALYSIS   lex (CP)

Name

lex—generate programs to do lexical analysis of text

Synopsis

lex [−rctvn] [*filename*] . . .

Description

lex generates programs to do simple lexical analysis of text by (1) dividing input strings of characters into tokens which match specified patterns and (2) executing routines in response to the detection of such tokens. The overall program created is yylex(). The lex library supplies a main() which calls it.

The lex command creates a file, lex.yy.c. After compilation and loading of libraries, lex.yy.c copies input to output unless a specified pattern is found in the input. In this case, the matching character string is stored in yytext[], a character array. The number of characters in a matching string is counted and stored in yyleng. Matching strings are left in yytext[ ].

Any string that starts with a blank is treated as C text and is copied. If such a string precedes %%, it is copied to the definitions area of lex.yy.c (see below). Lines that start with a nonblank character and precede %% designate the string on the left as the remainder of the line. Such a line can be called out later by surrounding it with {}.

Input to lex consists of lex source (the lex specification). The lex specification has three sections: a definitions section (optional), followed by a rules section (mandatory), followed by user subroutines (optional).

Definition Section

The definition section may contain abbreviations, external definitions, #include statements, and #define statements. Abbreviations represent regular expressions to be used in the rules section. These abbreviations simplify references to digits, letters, and blanks. Each abbreviation begins on the left end of a line and, after one or more spaces, is followed by its definition. For example, D [0-9] substitutes D for [0-9] in any references to [0-9] in the rules or subroutine sections.

External definitions have the same purpose and form as in C. The special #include file, y.tab.h, may contain #defines for token names.

The user may set table sizes (in the definitions section) for a finite state machine, using the following definitions:

%a *n* sets the number of state transitions to *n* (default 2000).

%e *n* sets the number of parse tree nodes to *n* (default 1000).

%k *n* sets the number of packed character classes to *n* (default 2500).

%n *n* sets the number of states to *n* (default 500).

%o *n* sets the size of output array to *n* (default 3000).

%p *n* sets the number of positions to *n* (default 2500).

Using any of the above definitions implies using the −v option below unless the −n option is used instead.

Rules Section

The rules section begins with a %% delimiter. The section uses operators, delimiters, and characters to describe patterns to be sought in the input and the action to be taken when the specified pattern is found. The operators and delimiters have the following meanings:

[ ] means any single character from the string within the brackets. Ranges of alphabetic or numeric characters are designated using a hyphen, −. For example, [0-9] means any one of the 10 decimal digits.

{} is used as in the C language. The braces delimit an action extending over several lines of C code. Curly braces do not imply parentheses; only string substitution is performed.

* means zero or more occurrences of the preceding expression.

+ means one or more occurrences of the preceding expression.

? means zero or one occurrence of the preceding expression, i.e., the preceding expression is optional.

. means any ASCII character except a newline.

( ) is used for grouping.

| is used for separating alternatives. It has a lower precedence than *****, **?**, **+**, or concatenation.

reg{*a*,*b*} means between *a* and *b* occurrences of a regular expression, *reg*. It has a lower precedence than *****, **?**, **+**, or concatenation but a higer precedence than **|**.

^ preceding an expression lets the expression match a pattern only if a newline immediately precedes the expression.

$ is equivalent to **\ n**. It indicates the end of a line, a special trailing context. For example, **[ ] + $;** causes all spaces at the end of a line to be ignored.

/ indicates a trailing context. The part of the expression up to the slash (**/**) is sent to *yytext*, but the part of the expression following **/** must be present in the input stream.

" preceding and following an operator character allows its use as an ordinary character.

**** preceding an operator character allows its use as an ordinary character. For example, **** uses **** as an ordinary character, not as an escape character.

The rules section must end with a **%%** delimiter if a user subroutine section follows the rules section. If no **%%** is given, the rule section extends to the end of the program.

User Subroutines Section

Any user-defined routine may be put in the user subroutine section, but user-defined versions of input( ), unput(c), and output(c) are particularly likely to be placed there.

Three subroutines defined as macros are required: input( ) to read a character, unput(c) to replace a character in input after reading it, and output(c) to output a character.

The macros input( ) and output(c) use yyin to read from and yyout to write, with stdin and stdout as default input and output, respectively. The standard streams can be overridden.

Several functions allow sequences of characters to be treated in more than one way. The yymore( ) routine appends matching strings to those already in yytext[ ] instead of overwriting them. This facilitates handling a matching string that is a substring of another matching string. The yyless(n) function resets the endpoint of the matching string to the nth character of yytext[ ], i.e., it pushes back (yyleng-n) characters into the input stream (yyleng, an external int variable gives the length of yytext). When the REJECT function appears on the right side of a rule, it causes a match to be rejected and the next suitable match to be executed instead.

Options and Arguments

-c causes C program actions in response to expressions.

-n suppresses the -v summary.

-Q{y|n} prints version information to output file lex.yy.c if -Qy is specified. The default, -Qn, causes no version information to be output.

-t writes lex.yy.c to standard output.

-V prints out the version of lex on the standard output.

-v prints a two-line summary of statistics about input.

filename holds character strings and expressions to be analyzed and C source code to be executed when specified expressions are detected. The default file is standard input. Multiple files are treated as a single file, and all files must be specified after any lex options are specified.

See Also

yacc (CP), lex chapter (AT&T 1990g)

---

lint (CP)   **C DEBUGGING AIDS**   **lint (CP)**

Name

lint—check C programs for bad features

Synopsis

lint [*option*] ... *filenames* ... *library-descrip tor(s)*

Description

lint analyzes C program files, trying to find inconsistencies that may be bugs, unportable features, or features that waste resources. It detects automatic variables that are declared but not used, logical variables whose values do not change, loops entered elsewhere than at the top, and unreachable statements. It detects differences between the data type expected from a function and the data type actually returned. It also detects differences between the number of arguments (and/or their data type) expected by a function and the number of arguments (and/or their data type) actually received. It finds functions whose returned values are not used and functions that return values at some places but not others.

lint processes .c, .ln, and llib-lx.ln files specified by lx (see -lx below) in the order in which their specifications occur on the command line. lint appends llib-lc.ln to the list of files specified on the command line.

The symbol "lint" should be regarded as a reserved word in code to be checked by lint because the preprocessor symbol "lint" is defined to permit code to be altered or removed before lint checking.

Lint Comments

Several C language comments in source code can change the behavior of lint. The comments are as follows:

/*ARGUSEDn*/ causes lint to check only the first n arguments for usage (the default for n is 0). This comment acts like the -v option (described below) on the next function.

/*CONSTCOND*/ or /*CONSTANTCOND*/ or /*CONSTANTCONDITION*/ suppresses warnings about any constant operands in the next expression.

/*EMPTY*/ suppresses warnings about a null statement that is a consequence statement of an if statement. Put this directive after the test expression but before the semicolon. This directive is for use when a valid else statement follows an empty if statement. It suppresses warnings that would otherwise occur when an else consequence statement is empty.

/*FALLTHRU*/ or /*FALLTHROUGH*/ suppresses warnings about fallthrough to either a case or default labeled statement. Put this directive immediately before the label.

/*LINTED [message]*/ suppresses intrafile warnings other than those about unused variables or functions. Put this directive on the line immediately before the place where the intrafile warning occurred. Notice that the -k option below changes the action of this directive. Use this directive with the -s option in filtering after lint execution.

/*LINTLIBRARY*/ acts like the -v and -x options. When placed at the beginning of a file, it suppresses warnings about unused functions and function arguments in the file. See the -y option below.

/*NOTREACHED*/ suppresses warnings about code that is unreachable. Put this comment after calls to functions such as exit (Peterson 1991a).

/*PRINTFLIKE*/ causes lint to interpret the nth argument of a function as a printf format string to be used in checking the remaining arguments. lint checks the first (n - 1) arguments as usual.

/*PROTOLIB*/ makes lint treat function declarations as function definitions if *n* is not 0. The /*LINTLIBRARY*/ directive must be used if this directive is used. lint treats function declarations normally if *n* is 0.

/*SCANFLIKE*/ causes lint to interpret the *n*th argument of a function as a scanf format string to be used in checking the remaining arguments. lint checks the first (*n* - 1) arguments as usual.

/*VARARGS*n**/ suppresses checking for variable numbers of arguments in the function declaration it precedes. lint checks the data types of the first *n* arguments. If *n* is missing, it is assumed to be 0. Use an ellipsis terminator in the function declaration in new or updated code.

Options and Arguments

The options below may be used in any number and in any order, and filenames may be intermixed with options. lint warns about any option it does not recognize but otherwise ignores such an option.

Select the Amount of lint Information to Be Output

Suppress lint Warning Messages

−a suppresses warnings about assignment of long values to variables that are not long.

−b suppresses warnings about unreachable break statements.

−m suppresses warnings about external symbols that might be declared static.

−u suppresses warnings about external variables and functions defined and not used or used and not defined.

−v suppresses warnings about unused arguments of functions.

−x suppresses warnings about variables referred to by external declarations but never used.

Augment lint Information Output

−F prints pathnames of files in addition to the filename. The default is that filenames are printed without pathnames.

−k changes the action of /*LINTED [*message*]*/ directives, causing lint to print an additional message that contains *message*. Otherwise, lint suppresses warning messages for code following a /*LINTED [*message*]*/ directive.

−s generates a one-line diagnostic for each error. Otherwise, if −s is not specified, lint collects warnings about errors in included files and prints the error messages after it processes all source files.

−V writes the product name and release number to standard error output.

Select Other lint *Behavior*

−c causes lint to create (as a product of lint's first pass) a separate .ln file for each .c file specified on the command line. lint does not check these .ln files for interfunction compatibility. If −c is not specified, lint collects information from all input files and checks it for consistency, after which it prints a question mark (?) following the source filename if it is not clear whether a warning is caused by an error in the source file or in one of its included files.

If −c is specified, lint ignores the .ln and llib-lx.ln files. If −c is not specified, lint's second pass checks the .ln and llib-lx.ln files for mutual compatibility.

Ordinarily, lint is invoked once for each source file, with each of these invocations creating a .ln file corresponding to a .c file. lint then outputs all the messages pertaining to that source file. After lint has processed each separate source file, it can be invoked again (without −c) to list each .ln file with the necessary options. This prints each interfile inconsistency, permitting make to be used to lint only those source files that have been altered since the last lint.

The −c option suppresses the −o option.

−D is the −D option of the compiler. See cc (CP).

−g is the −g option of the compiler, recognized but ignored by lint. See cc (CP).

−h suppresses heuristic tests that try to find bugs, improve style, or reduce waste.

−I*dir* causes lint to search for #include files in the directory *dir* before it searches the current directory and/or the standard location for #include files.

−L*dir* makes lint search for its libraries in *dir* before seacrhing the standard library location.

−l*x* includes the lint library, llib-lx.ln. For example, −lm on the command line causes a lint version of the math library, llib-lm.ln, to be included. −l*x* enables lint to reference local lint libraries; these libraries must be in the assumed directory. lint continues to use the default lint library even if −l*x* is specified.

−n suppresses checks for compatibility with the standard or portable lint library.

−O is the −O option of the compiler, recognized but ignored by lint. See cc (CP).

−o *x* causes the lint library, llib-lx.ln, which lint creates and later uses in its second pass, to be saved in lliblx.ln. See the −c option above. Use the −v option if the source files for the lint library are external references. Use the −x option to create llib-lx.ln without producing

warning messages about unused external variables. The effects of options −v
and x can be produced by the use of lint comments described above.

−p enforces stricter checking. It tries to check portabilty to other dialects of
C. The option also truncates all nonexternal names to 8 characters and all external
names to 6 characters and one case.

−R*file* copies a .ln file to *file* for cxref (CP) to use in building a
cross-reference table.

−U is the −U option of the compiler. See cc (CP).

−W*file* copies a .ln file to *file* for cflow (CP) to use in charting
external references.

−Xa is a cc (CP) command line option.

−Xc is a cc (CP) command line option.

−Xt is a cc (CP) command line option.

−y specifies that files being processed by lint will be treated as if a
/*LINTLIBRARY*/ directive has been used. A /*LINTLIBRARY*/
directive ordinarily is used in creating a lint library.

filenames are the files to be checked by lint. The *filenames* must
end with .c for C source files or with .ln for files generated by an earlier use
of lint with either the −c or the −o option. Files with .ln extensions are
analogous to object files (.o extensions) created by the compiler from input
files with .c extensions. Files with other extensions cause warnings and are not
processed.

Files

LIBDIR is the directory where lint libraries required by the −l*x* option
must be located.

LIBDIR/lint[12] contains the first and second passes of lint.

LIBDIR/llib-lc.ln contains C library function declarations (binary
format; see LIBDIR/llib-lc for source code).

LIBPATH/llib-lm.ln contains math library function declarations (binary format; see LIBDIR/llib/−lm for source code).

TMPDIR ordinarily is /var/tmp, but setting the environment variable
TMPDIR can redefine it [see tmpnam (Peterson 1992a)].

TMPDIR/*lint* contains temporary files.

LIBDIR ordinarily is /ccs/lib.

LIBPATH ordinarily is /usr/ccs/lib:usr/lib.

See Also

cc (CP), make (CP)
lint chapter (AT&T 1990g)

Name

lorder—get an ordering relation for an object library

Synopsis

lorder *filenames* ...

Description

lorder lists pairs of object files or archive member names. The first file of each pair refers to external variables that are defined in the second file.

The output from lorder may be sent to tsort (CP) to find a library ordering allowing one-pass access by ld (CP). Although this may make link edit access somewhat more efficient, it is not required because the link editor, ld (CP), can make multiple passes over any archive that is in the portable archive format.

The following command sequence builds a new library, using existing .o files:

ar -cr *library* 'lorder *.o | tsort'

Options and Arguments

lorder has no options, but input files are specified on the command line as follows:

filenames is one or more object or library archive files [compare with ar (CP)]. If there is more than one input file, any archive file or object suffix is acceptable. If there is only one input file, its suffix must be .o.

Files

TMPDIR/*symref contains temporary files.
TMPDIR/*symdef contains temporary files.
TMPDIR ordinarily is /var/tmp, but it can be redefined by changing the environment variable TMPDIR. See tmpnam (Peterson 1992a).

See Also

ar (CP), ld (CP), tsort (CP), ar (F), tmpnam (Peterson 1992a)

lprof (CP)   **PROFILING**   **lprof (CP)**

Name

lprof—display line-by-line code execution count

Synopsis

lprof [-p] [-s] [-x] [[-I *incdir*]] [[-r*srcfile*]] [-c*cntfile*]
[-o *prog*] [-V]
lprof -m *file1.cnt file2.cnt*. . . [[*filen.cnt*]] [-T] -d
*dstfile.cnt*ls

Description

lprof is a run-time tool for finding the most frequently executed parts of source code on a line-by-line basis. It can find code that is never executed, and it can merge data files.

lprof has limitations; if code is optimized, it cannot be profiled. Profiling has precedence over optimization if both are specified.

lprof prints (by default) a source listing of files whose names are stored in the symbol table of the executable file. Each line of the listing is preceded by its line number in the source file and by a count of the number of times the line was executed (see -r *srcfile* below).

If a program, *prog*, is compiled using the -ql option of cc (CP), lprof can process a profile file (*prog*.cnt is the default name of the profile file). The -ql option inserts code to record the run-time results and write profile data to a profile file at the end of execution.

If -ql is specified when a shared object is created, the shared object may be profiled. At run time for a dynamically linked executable, one profile file is created for each profiled shared object linked to the dynamic executable. This enables one report to be created that covers multiple different executions of a common library. For instance, if two profiled programs, *proga* and *progb*, use a library, executing these programs will create two profile files that cannot be combined unless three conditions are met. First, the library they use must have been built as a shared object. Second, *proga* and *progb* must have been built as profiled, dynamically linked executables. Third, *proga* and *progb* must be run with the merge option (see below), producing three profile files, one of which (lib.so.cnt) contains the libx profile information from both profile runs.

PROFOPTS Environment Variable

PROFOPTS, an environment variable, controls profiling at run time. PROFOPTS is a list of run-time options separated by commas. When it is about to terminate execution, a shared object or program being profiled examines PROFOPTS in order to decide what to do with profile data.

If PROFOPTS is a null string, no profiling data are saved. If PROFOPTS is not defined, profile data are saved in a file in the current directory; the default name of the file is *prog*.cnt. The following run-time options determine the disposition of profile data:

dir = *directory* puts the profile data file in directory *directory*. Otherwise, the profile data are put in whatever directory is current at the end of execution.

file = *filename* specifies *filename* as the name of the file of profile data created by the profiled program. Otherwise, the default *filename* is used. See the −c option.

merge = [y|n] causes the data file to be overwritten after each run and files not to be merged if merge = n (the default). If merge = y, data files will be merged after each run.

The merge fails if the program has been recompiled, and profile data are left in TMPDIR.

msg = [y|n] sends a message to stderr stating that profile data are being saved when msg = y (the default). If msg = n, only profiling error messages are printed.

pid = [y|n] causes the name of the profile data file to include the process ID of the profiled program if pid = y, enabling the creation of different profile data files for programs calling fork (Peterson 1991a). The default name of the file is used if pid = n. The −c option must be used in order for lprof to create its profile report; otherwise, the default will fail.

Options and Arguments

The following options may be specified in any order and may be combined:

−c *cntfile* makes lprof use *cntfile* as the profile input file, instead of prog.cnt. In order for lprof to create its profile report, −c must be specified with lprof if the file = *filename* environment variable was used at run time. Otherwise, the default will fail.

−d *dstfile* is described in option −m below. The −d and −m options must be used together when *lprof* is used to merge data files.

−I *incdir* makes lprof search for source or header files in directory *incdir*, as well as in the current directory, and in the standard directory for #include files, often /usr/include. More than one directory can be specified on a command line by using more than one −I *incdir*.

−m *file1*.cnt *file2*.cnt . . . [[*filem*.cnt]] sums the execution counts for each corresponding line in *file1*.cnt through *filen*.cnt, accumulating data from several profiling runs. The results are put in *dstfile*.cnt, and the −d *dstfile*.cnt option must be used with the −m option. If *dstfile*.cnt already exists, its previous contents are destroyed. Each input file must contain profiling data for the same program (but see the −T option).

−o *prog* substitutes *prog* for the name used when the profile file was created. If the executable file or the profile file has been moved, it is necessary to use −o because the program name that is stored in the profile file contains the relative path.

−p prints a listing showing each line of code preceded by its line number and the number of times it was executed. If −p is used with −s, both the source listing and summary information are printed.

−r *srcfile* causes only those source files specified by −r *srcfile* to be printed, instead of all source files. This option is to be used only with the −p option. Multiple files can be specified with one −r option.

−s prints a summary showing the percentage of lines of code executed per function.

−T overrides the time stamp, allowing files to be merged even if their time stamps do not match.

−V prints the version number of lprof on the standard error.

−x prints only the line number of any line executed instead of printing the execution count for each line. Lines not executed are printed, preceded by a line number and a [U].

prog.cnt is the profile file (*prog*.cnt by default) created by the profiled program prog.

prog is the program that creates a profile file that lprof interprets.

Files

prog.cnt contains profile data.

TMPDIR ordinarily is /var/tmp; however, it can be redefined by changing the environment variable, TMPDIR [*tmpnam* (Peterson 1992a)].

See Also

cc (CP), prof (CP), fork (Peterson 1991a), tmpnam (Peterson 1992a) lprof chapter (AT&T 1990g)

| **m4 (CP)** | **MACRO PREPROCESSING** | **m4 (CP)** |

Name

m4—macroprocessor

Synopsis

m4 [*options*] [*filenames*]

Description

m4 is a macro processor for assembler, C, and other computer languages. It processes argument files in the order in which they are specified, writing the processed text to the standard output.

m4 processes each file as it encounters the filename on the command line. If no filenames are specified or if a filename is −, m4 reads the standard input, looking for filenames.

Macro names may consist of alphabetic characters, digits, and the underscore character, __. The first character may not be a digit.

Macro calls have the following form:

name(*arg1*, *arg2*, . . . *argn*)

No spaces may occur between *name* and (, the leftmost parenthesis. If there is an intervening space, m4 assumes that the macro being called has no argu ments.

When m4 collects arguments, it ignores leading unquoted blanks, tabs, and newlines. Single quotes, left and right, enclose quoted strings. The value of any quoted string is the string, stripped of quotes. (See the built-in macro changequote below for a description of quote characters.)

When m4 recognizes a macro name, it collects the macro's arguments by searching for a matching right parenthesis. If fewer macro arguments are supplied than are specified by the macro definition, the trailing arguments are treated as null arguments. m4 continues evaluating macro arguments during the collection of arguments. The value of a macro is pushed back onto the input stream and rescanned after argument collection. Any commas or right parentheses encountered within the value of a nested call have the same effect as those within the original text.

Built-in Macros

Nearly three dozen built-in macros are available with the *m4* command. These may be redefined, but this causes the original meaning of such a macro to be forgotten. Macros have null values unless otherwise specified.

GET/OMIT Debugging Information

errprint() sends its arguments to the diagnostic output file.

dumpdef() prints names and definitions for specified items. All are printed if no arguments are specified.

traceon( ) turns on tracing for all macros if no arguments are specified. Otherwise, only the named macros are traced. A call to traceoff is required to untrace any macro specified by traceon.

traceoff( ) turns tracing off, both globally and for specified macros.

Manipulate Macro Arguments/Strings

changecom(arg1, arg2) disables comments if no arguments are specified. Otherwise, the left and right comment markers are changed from the default values of # and newline, respectively, if changecom has two arguments. If changecom has only one argument, the argument becomes the left marker and the right marker remains newline. Each comment marker may be up to 5 characters long.

changequote(arg1, arg2) changes argument quote symbols from the original values, ' ', to some other quote symbols, each up to 5 characters long. If no arguments are specified, the original quote symbols are restored.

decr(arg) returns the value of an argument after decrementing it by 1.

dnl( ) reads and discards the remaining characters of a line, including the newline.

eval(expr, rad, dig) has three arguments: an arithmetic expression, the radix for the result (octal and hex numbers may be specified as in C), and an argument specifying a minimum number of digits in the result. The macro uses 32-bit arithmetic to evaluate the expression. Expressions may contain arithmetic operators: $\%$, $+$, $-$, $*$, $/$, $\char`^$ (exponentiation); bitwise operators: $\&$, $|$, $\char`^$, and $\tilde{}$; relational operators; and parentheses.

ifelse(string1, string2, string3 . . .) permits conditional testing of its arguments. If string1 is identical to string2, then the value of ifelse is string3. Otherwise, if there are five or more arguments, testing is repeated with arguments 4, 5, 6, and 7. But if string1 and string2 are not identical and no fourth string is present, the macro value is null.

incr(arg) interprets its initial digit-string argument as a decimal number, increments it by 1, and returns that value.

index(string1, string2) returns the position in string1 where the string2 starts (zero origin is assumed). If string2 is not present, the macro returns -1.

len(arg) returns the character length of its argument.

shift(arg1, arg2, . . . argn) returns all its arguments except the first. These arguments are quoted, have commas inserted between them, and are pushed back. The quotes nullify the effect of an extra scan that will be performed later.

substr(string, start, length) returns a substring of string which begins at start and is length long.

translit(string, char, replace) replaces each character in

string which matches a character in *char* with the corresponding character in *replace*. For example, `translit(cat, cats, DOGS)` returns DOG.

Manipulate Macro Definitions

`define(`*name, substitution*`)` has the following arguments: The first macro argument, argument 0, is the macro name. The second argument of `define` becomes the value of the macro whose name is the first argument.

Each instance of `$n` in the replacement text is replaced by the *n*th argument; *n* is an integer. `$#` is replaced by the number of macro arguments. `$*` is replaced by a comma-separated list of arguments. `$@` is replaced by a comma-separated list of arguments; each argument is quoted. Argument 0 is the macro name.

`defn(`*arg1, arg2,* . . .`)` can rename macros. It returns the quoted definition of its argument(s).

`ifdef(`*arg1, arg2, arg3*`)` returns a value equal to *arg2* if *arg1* is defined; otherwise, it returns a value equal to *arg3*. The value is null if there is no *arg3*. The predefined word `unix` can be used with `m4`.

`undefine( )` deletes the definition of the macro specified in its argument.

`popdef(arg1, arg2,` . . .`)` deletes the current definition of its arguments. This brings the previous definition, if any, into view.

`pushdef(`*arg1, arg2,* . . .`)` works like `define( )` but also saves any previous definition.

Manipulate Streams

`divert(`*digit-string*`)` diverts the current output stream to the stream specified by *digit-string* (`m4` has up to 10 output streams, numbered 0–9). Final output consists of the concatenation of streams in numeric order. Output diverted to streams other than streams 0–9 is thrown away.

`undivert( )` immediately outputs text from diversions specified by arguments, or from all diversions if none is specified. Undiverting throws the diverted text away. Text can be undiverted to another diversion.

`divnum( )` returns the value of the current stream (usually it is 0–9; see `divert` above).

Manipulate Process Environment

`include(`*file*`)` returns the contents of *file*.

`maketmp( )` puts the process ID of the current process in string *XXXXX* in the macro's arguments.

`m4exit( )` causes exit from `m4`. The exit code is argument 1 if specified. Otherwise, it is 0.

`m4wrap( )` pushes argument 1 back at the final EOF.

sinclude( ) is the same as include, except that m4 silently continues processing if a specified file cannot be found.

syscmd( ) executes the UNIX system command specified by the macro's first argument. For example, syscmd(date) executes the UNIX date command and includes it in m4 output.

sysval( ) gives the return code from the most recent execution of syscmd.

Options and Arguments

Leading Options

The following options must precede any filenames or −U or −D options specified on the command line:

−e specifies interactive operation with unbuffered output. Interrupts are ignored.

−Bint sets the size of the argument-collection and push-back buffers to some other value than the default (4096).

−Hint sets the size of the symbol table hash array to int, a prime value (default is 199).

−Sint sets the size of the call stack to int (default is 100). Macros require three slots. Nonmacro arguments require one.

−s enables line sync output for the C preprocessor, i.e., #line . . .

−Tint sets the size of the token buffer to int (default is 512).

Trailing Options and Arguments

If any of the following options and filenames is specified, it must follow any leading options that are specified.

−Dname[= val] defines the value of name to be val if val is specified. Otherwise, name is null.

filenames specifies input files. Input comes from the standard input if no file is specified or if filenames is −.

−Uname causes name to be undefined.

See Also

as (CP), cc (CP)

| make (CP) | SOFTWARE VERSION CONTROL | make (CP) |

Name

make—maintain, update, or regenerate program groups

Synopsis

make [-f *makefile*] [-e] [-i] [-k] [-n] [-p] [-q] [-r] [-s] [t]
[*filenames*]

Description

make automates the creation, maintenance, and updating of groups of programs. It uses several kinds of information: a description file supplied by the
user, filenames, dates that files were last modified, and built-in rules. Using
these elements, make executes commands specified in *makefile* in order
to update target files selectively. Any target file is updated only if its dependents
are newer than it is. Any prerequisite files (dependencies) of a target are recur-
sively added to the list of targets. make treats missing files as being outdated.

Creating a makefile

makefiles, invoked with the -f option, contain instructions for updating
and re-creating programs. *makefiles* typically contain a series of entries
that specify dependencies. The first line of each entry is a blank-separated list
of target files followed by a colon (:) and then by a list of prerequisite files or
dependencies (which may be a null list). If include comprises the first seven
letters of a line in *makefile* and is followed by a blank or tab, make treats
the remainder of the line as a filename and reads the filename after the substitution
of any macros (see the "Macros" section below). Any text following a semicolon
(;) and any following lines that start with a tab are shell commands that need
to be executed to update the target file. Shell commands can extend from a first
line to a second line if a backslash (\ ) and a newline mark the end of the first
line. For example, the sequence

echo s \
db

will display sdb.

Commands that the shell executes directly, for example, cd (CP), will not
work across newlines in make.

Any nonempty line starting with a character other than sharp (#) or tab begins
a new macro definition or dependency. A *makefile* can have comments,
including embedded \ newline sequences. These are delimited by sharp (#)
and newline.

Command lines in *makefile* are executed one at a time. Each is executed
by its own shell. The SHELL environment variable can specify the shell that
make uses to execute the commands it finds. Otherwise, the default shell is
/usr/bin/sh.

The first 1 or 2 characters in a command line may be as follows:
– causes make to ignore any errors. This is one of three conditions that can cause make to ignore any errors. In addition, any command that returns a nonzero status terminates make unless the −i option is used (see below) or .IGNORE is included in the makefile.

@ causes a line not to be printed when it is executed (see the makefile directive, .SILENT, and the −s option).

−@ causes make to ignore any errors and suppresses printing of a line when it is executed.

@− causes make to ignore any errors and suppresses printing of a line when it is executed.

Command arguments are evaluated as follows: First, macros (arguments having equal signs embedded) are examined and all assignments are made. Second, make examines option arguments. Finally, make assumes that any remaining arguments are the names of targets, and it processes the arguments from left to right.

The first name in the description file that starts with a character other than a period is taken to be a target if make finds no target arguments on the command line.

Macros

The makefile may contain user-defined macros defined by entries having the form string1 = string2. Occurrences of $(string1[:subst1 = [subst2]]) are replaced by string2. Parentheses are required if the macro name is not a single character or if there is a substitution sequence. [:subst1 = [subst2]] is the (optional) substitution sequence. Strings in such substitutions are delimited by blanks, newline characters, tabs, or beginnings of lines. string2 consists of all characters up to an unescaped newline or comment character. All nonoverlapping occurrences of string1 are replaced by string2.

Makefile Example

The following example illustrates a simple makefile in which a target program, prog, depends on three object files, x.o, y.o, and z.o, which in turn are dependent on their source files, x.c, y.c, and z.c, and on an include file used by all three, incl.h:

```
#comments here
prog: x.o y.o z.o
    cc x.o y.o z.o −o prog
x.o: incl.h x.c
    cc −c x.c
```

```
y.o: incl.h y.c
    cc -c y.c
z.o: incl.h z.c
    cc -c z.c
```

Internal Macros

Internal macros are useful in writing rules for generating targets. There are five of these macros, as follows:

$% expands to the name of a library member. It is evaluated only when the target is an archive library member like lib(file.o). Here $@ evaluates to lib and $% evaluates to the library member file.o.

$* expands to the filename part of the current dependent, but without the suffix. It is evaluated for inference rules only.

$< expands to the filename of the module that is outdated compared to the target dependent file. It is evaluated only for inference rules or for the .DEFAULT directive (see .DEFAULT below).

$? is evaluated when explicit rules from *makefile* are evaluated. It expands to the string of filenames of all dependents that are younger than the current target.

$@ expands to the complete pathname of the current target. It is evaluated for explicitly named dependencies only.

Four of the above macros may take either of two alternative forms. If D is appended to $%, $*, $<, or $@, i.e., if they become $(%D), $(*D), $(<D), or $(@D), respectively, the meaning changes to "directory part," i.e., the macro expansion is to the directory part of the target name. Analogously, if F is appended to any of these four macros, the expansion is to the file part of the name. If no directory part exists, ./ is generated. The $? macro cannot have these alternative forms.

Environment Variables

make reads the environment and processes any environment variables as macro definitions. make interacts with the environment through an environment variable, MAKEFLAGS, that make maintains. MAKEFLAGS consists of all the input flag arguments collected together into a string (but without minus signs). MAKEFLAGS is exported, so it is usable by commands that make invokes. Any command line assignments and flags update the string in MAKEFILE. If the MAKEFLAGS environment variable is absent or null, the internal make variable, MAKEFLAGS, is set to the null string. Otherwise, each keyletter except -f, -p, and -r in MAKEFLAGS is processed as an input flag argument.

Upon execution, make assigns macro definitions in the following order of precedence:

TABLE 1-4.   Filename suffixes recognized by make.

Suffix	File
.o	Object file
.c ~	C source file
.c	SCCS C source file
.f ~	FORTRAN source file
.f	SCCS FORTRAN file
.s ~	Assembler source file
.s	SCCS assembler source file
.y ~	yacc source file
.y	SCCS yacc source file
.l ~	lex source file
.l	SCCS lex source grammar
.h ~	Header file
.h	SCCS header file
.sh ~	Shell file
.sh	SCCS shell file
.C ~	C + + source file
.C	SCCS C + + source file
.L ~	C + + source grammar for lex
.L	SCCS C + + source grammar for lex
.Y ~	C + + source grammar for yacc
.Y	SCCS C + + source grammar for yacc

1. make read the internal rules (see below).
2. make reads the environment, treating environment variables as macro definitions and marking them as exported.
3. make reads *makefile*(s). Assignments found in *makefile*(s) override the environment. What the user sees is what the user gets, unless the −e command line flag is used to tell make that the environment overrides the assignments in *makefile*(s).

Suffixes and their associated rules in *makefile*(s) override any identical suffixes in internal rules (see the following section).

Suffixes and Internal Rules

Some files obviously depend on other files. For example, files with .o suffixes are derived from other files that have suffixes such as .s or .c. If *makefile* contains no explicit update command for such a file, make still may cause a dependent file to be compiled in order to build a specified target, because make examines the file suffix and chooses an internal rule that tells it that compilation is required. The source file rules.c contains internal rules that govern such

TABLE 1-5.   Predefined macros recognized by make.

```
AR = ar
ARFLAGS = -rv
AS = as
ASFLAGS =
BUILD = build
CC = cc
CFLAGS = -O
C + +C = CC
C + +FLAGS = -O
F77 = f77
FFLAGS = -O
GET = get
GFLAGS =
LEX = lex
LFLAGS =
LD = ld
LDFLAGS =
MAKE = make
MAKEFLAGS =
YACC = yacc
YFLAGS =
$ = $
```

activity. These rules may be modified. In order to print the rules in a form that can be recompiled, execute the following command:

$$\texttt{make -fp - 2>/dev/null </dev/null}$$

Some internal rules contain tildes (˜). Each ˜ refers to an SCCS file see **sccs file** (AT&T 1990m)]. The ˜ is used because the use of **.s** in SCCS files is incompatible with **make**'s usage of suffixes. A ˜ converts a file reference into an SCCS file reference.

The list of filename suffixes that **make** recognizes is given in Table 1-4. The list is the dependency list for the name **.SUFFIXES**. The order of the list is significant because the list is scanned from left to right. Multiple lists of suffixes accumulate. The first name for which both a rule and a file exist is regarded as a prerequisite. If **.SUFFIXES** is given without dependencies, it clears the dependency list. To print the suffixes, execute **make -fp - 2>/dev/null </dev/null**.

Table 1-5 shows the predefined macros that **make** recognizes. These macros specify some substitutions in inference rules.

Table 1-6 shows single-suffix rules that **make** uses. Single-suffix rules tell how to build **y** from **y.c**. In this case, the other suffix is, in effect, null. These

TABLE 1-6.   Single-suffix rules that govern make

Suffix	Action
.c:	$(CC) $(CFLAGS) $(LDFLAGS) −o $@ $<
.c~:	$(GET) $(GFLAGS) $<
	$(CC) $(CFLAGS) $(LDFLAGS) −o $* $*.c
	−rm −f $*.c
.s:	$(AS) $(AFLAGS) −o $@ $<
.s~:	$(GET) $(GFLAGS) $<
	$(AS) $(AFLAGS) −o $@ $*.s
	rm −f $*.s
.sh:	cp $< $@; chmod 0777 $@
.sh~:	$(GET) $(GFLAGS) $<
	cp $*.sh $*; chmod 0777 $@
	rm −f $*.sh
.f:	$(F77) $(FFLAGS) $(LDFLAGS) −o $@ $<
.f~:	$(GET) $(GFLAGS) $<
	$(F77) $(FFLAGS) −o $@ $(LDFLAGS) $*.f
	−rm −f $*.f
.C~:	$(GET) $(GFLAGS) $<
	$(C++C) $(C++FLAGS) −o $@ $(LDFLAGS) $*.C
	rm −f $*.C
.C:	$(C++C) $(C++FLAGS) −o $@ $(LDFLAGS) $<

rules are used for building targets when only one source file exists (e.g., simple C programs or shell procedures).

make also recognizes the double-suffix rules shown in Table 1-7.

Libraries

Any dependency or target name containing parentheses is treated as the name of an archive library. Any string within the parentheses refers to a member within the archive library. If the LIB macro is defined, either $(LIB)(file.o) or lib(file.o) designates an archive library with file.o as a member. The expression (lib(filea.o fileb.o filec.o) is not permitted.

Rules for archive libraries look like .YY.a. The archive member name is made from the suffix YY. The current implementation requires that YY be different from the suffix of the archive member. Thus it is impossible to build lib(filea.o) from filea.o.

Inference Rules

Default inference rules can use macros to include optional matter in commands. For example, such rules can use macros CFLAGS, LFLAGS, and YFLAGS to specify compiler options to cc (CP), lex (CP), and yacc (CP), respectively.

TABLE 1-7.   Double-suffix rules that govern make

Suffix	Action
.c˜.c .y˜.y .l˜.l .s˜.s .sh˜.sh .h˜.h .f˜.f	
.C˜.C .Y˜.Y .L˜.L.	
(Any of these preceding pairs of suffixes causes the following action:)	
	$(GET) $(GFLAGS) $<
.c.a:	$(CC) -c $(CFLAGS) $<
	$(AR) $(ARFLAGS) $@ $*.o
	rm -f $*.o
.c˜.a:	$(GET) $(GFLAGS) $<
	$(CC) -c $(CFLAGS) $*.c
	$(AR) $(ARFLAGS) $@ $*.o
	rm -f $*.[co]
.c.o:	$(CC) $(CFLAGS) -c $<
The following rule transforms an SCCS C source file into an object file:)	
.c˜.o:	$(GET) $(GFLAGS) $<
	$(CC) $(CFLAGS) -c $*.c
	-rm -f $*.c
.y.c:	$(YACC) $(YFLAGS) $<
	mv y.tab.c $@
.y˜.c:	$(GET) $(GFLAGS) $<
	$(YACC) $(YFLAGS) $*.y
	mv y.tab.c $*.c
	-rm -f $*.y
.y.o:	$(YACC) $(YFLAGS) $<
	$(CC) $(CFLAGS) -c y.tab.c
	rm -f y.tab.c
	mv y.tab.o $@
.y˜.o:	$(GET) $(GFLAGS) $<
	$(YACC) $(YFLAGS) $*.y
	$(CC) $(CFLAGS) -c y.tab.c
	-rm -f y.tab.c $*.y
	mv y.tab.o $*.o
.l.c:	$(LEX) $(LFLAGS) $<
	mv lex.yy.c $@
.l˜.c:	$(GET) $(GFLAGS) $<
	$(LEX) $(LFLAGS) $*.l
	mv lex.yy.c $@
	rm -f $*.l
.l.o:	$(LEX) $(LFLAGS) $<
	$(CC) $(CFLAGS) -c lex.yy.c
	rm -f lex.yy.c
	mv lex.yy.o $@

(continued)

TABLE 1-7.   *Continued*

Suffix	Action
.l˜.o:	$(GET) $(GFLAGS) $< $(LEX) $(LFLAGS) $*.l $(CC) $(CFLAGS) -c lex.yy.c rm -f lex.yy.c $*.l mv lex.yy.o $@
.s.a:	$(AS) $(ASFLAGS) -o $*.o $*.s $(AR) $(ARFLAGS) $@ $*.o
.s˜.a:	$(GET) $(GFLAGS) $< $(AS) $(ASFLAG) -o $*.o $*.s $(AR) $(ARFLAGS) $@ $*.o rm -f $*.[so]
.s.o:	$(AS) $(ASFLAG) -o $@ $<
.s˜.o:	$(GET) $(GFLAGS) $< $(AS) $(ASFLAG) -o $*.o $*.s rm -f $*.s
.f.a:	$(F77) $(FFLAGS) $(LDFLAGS) -c $*.f $(AR) $(ARFLAGS) $@ $*.o rm -f $*.o
.f˜.a:	$(GET) $(GFLAGS) $< $(F77) $(FFLAGS) -c $*.f $(AR) $(ARFLAGS) $@ $*.o rm -f $*.[fo]
.f.o .f˜.o:	$(F77) $(FFLAGS) -c $*.f $(GET) $(GFLAGS) $< $(F77) $(FFLAGS) -c $*.f rm -f $*.f
.C.a:	$(C++C) $(C++FLAGS) -c $< $(AR) $(ARFLAGS) $@ $*.o rm -f $*.o
.C˜.a:	$(GET) $(GFLAGS) $< $(C++C) $(C++FLAGS) -c $*.C $(AR) $(ARFLAGS) $@ $*.o rm -f $*.[Co]
.C.o: .C˜.o:	$(C++C) $(C++FLAGS) -c $< $(GET) $(GFLAGS) $< $(C++C) $(C++FLAGS) -c $*.C rm -f $*.C
.Y.C:	$(YACC) $(YFLAGS) $< mv y.tab.c $@
.Y˜.C:	$(GET) $(GFLAGS) $< $(YACC) $(YFLAGS) $*.Y mv y.tab.c $*.C rm -f $*.Y
.Y.o:	$(YACC) $(YFLAGS) $< $(C++C) $(C++FLAGS) -c y.tab.c rm -f y.tab.c mv y.tab.o $@

TABLE 1-7.   *Continued*

Suffix	Action
Y~.o:	$(GET) $(GFLAGS) $<
	$(YACC) $(YFLAGS) $*.Y
	$(C++C) $(C++FLAGS) -c y.tab.c
	rm -f y.tab.c $*.y
	mv y.tab.o $*.o
.L.C:	$(LEX) $(LFLAGS) $<
	mv lex.yy.c $@
.L.~.C:	$(GET) $(GFLAGS) $<
	$(LEX) $(LFLAGS) $*.L
	mv lex.yy.c $@
	rm -f $*.L
.L.o:	$(LEX) $(LFLAGS) $<
	$(C++C) $(C++FLAGS) -c lex.yy.c
	rm -f lex.yy.c
	mv lex.yy.o $@
.L~.o:	$(GET) $(GFLAGS) $<
	$(LEX) $(LFLAGS) $*.L
	$(C++C) $(C++FLAGS) -c lex.yy.c
	rm -f lex.yy.c $*.L
	mv lex.yy.o $@

Options and Arguments

Makefile Directives

Four different directives can be included in *makefile* to extend the options which make provides. make uses these directives as if they are targets. They are as follows:

.DEFAULT causes commands associated with the name .DEFAULT (if it exists) to be used if a file is to be created but there are no explicit commands or relevant built-in rules.

.IGNORE has the same effect as the -i option.

.PRECIOUS retains dependents of a target even if an interrupt or quit key is pressed.

.SILENT has the same effect as the -s option.

Options

make options are as follows:

-e causes environment variables to override assignments in *make files*.

−f *makefile* specifies the name of the description file. More than one −f *makefile* argument may be specified. If *makefile* is −, the standard input file is the description file. If −f is not specified, make searches for the description in the following files in the current directory, in the following order: makefile; Makefile; and the SCCS files, s.makefile and s.Makefile. If description files are present, their contents override built-in rules. This option cannot be specified in the MAKEFLAGS environment variable.

−i causes make to ignore error codes returned by commands invoked by make. Otherwise, such errors stop make. If the description file contains the fake target name .IGNORE, it has the same effect as this option. If a command inappropriately returns nonzero status, use −i to eliminate this difficulty.

−k stops processing the current command entry in *makefile* if it fails but continues processing other branches that do not depend on the current entry.

−n prints commands (including lines that start with @) but does not execute them (nonexecute mode). Nevertheless, a command line is always executed if it contains the string $(MAKE). Thus, make −n can be executed recursively on an entire software system because −n is put in the MAKEFLAGS environment variable (which always contains the current input options) and passed to subsequent invocations of $(MAKE), allowing *makefile* debugging without actual execution. This allows all of the makefiles of a software project to be debugged without actually doing anything.

−p prints all macro definitions and target descriptions (dependency lines) in the *makefile*. This option cannot be specified in the MAKEFLAGS environment variable.

−q causes make to return a status code of zero if a target file is up-to-date and nonzero if it is not.

−r suppresses the use of built-in rules for transforming a file with one suffix to a file with another suffix.

−s stops command lines from being printed before execution (silent mode). If the description file contains the fake target name .SILENT, it has the same effect as this option.

−t touches target files, changing the modification dates of the files without otherwise changing the files or executing commands.

names is ordinarily the name of a program. The name cannot contain the following characters: =, :, or @.

Files

```
[Mn]akefile
s.[Mn]akefile
/bin/sh
```

See Also

cc (CP), lex (CP), yacc (CP), cd (AT&T 1990q), printf (Peterson 1992a), sccsfile (F), sh (AT&T 1990q)
make chapter (AT&T 1990g)

mcs (CP)	OBJECT FILE MANIPULATION	mcs (CP)

Name

mcs—manipulate the comment section of an object file

Synopsis

mcs [-a *string*] [-c] [-d] [-n *name*] [-p] [-V] *object*(s)

Description

mcs adds data, compresses data, deletes data, or prints data that are in a section of an ELF object file. mcs also can print the contents of a section of a COFF file. However, mcs is unable to add to, delete from, or compress the contents of a section that is contained in a segment. The section which mcs manipulates is the .comment section by default.

mcs treats any archive [see ar (AT&T 1990m)] as a group of individual object files. For example, if -c is specified, mcs compresses the .comment section of each ELF file in the archive.

If mcs processes an archive file, it removes the archive symbol table unless -p is the only mcs option specified (see -p below). After the archive symbol table is removed, ld (CP) cannot link the archive until the symbol table is restored by executing ar with an -s option.

Options and Arguments

mcs cannot be used without options. It applies each option, in turn, to each specified file.

-a *string* causes *string* to be appended to the .comment section of a specified ELF *object* file(s). Any *string* containing blanks must be delimited by quotation marks.

-c compresses the .comment section of the specified ELF *object* file(s). It removes duplicate entries without disturbing the order of other entries.

-d removes the contents of the .comment section from the specified ELF *object* file(s). The header of the ELF *object* file(s) .comment section is removed, too.

−n *name* tells which section to access if the default section, .comment, is not specified.

−p prints (on standard output) the contents of the .comment section. mcs uses the name of the file from which a section was extracted to tag each section that mcs prints. If the section was extracted from an archive file, the tag has the format *filename*:[*string*]. If the section was extracted from any other file, the tag has the format *filename*:.

−V prints the version number of mcs on standard error.

object(s) are input object files for mcs to process.

Example

mcs −p *file* prints *file*'s .comment section.
mcs −c *file*.o compresses the .comment section of *file*.o.

Files

TMPDIR/mcs** contains temporary files.

TMPDIR ordinarily is /var/tmp. However, it can be redefined by changing the TMPDIR environment variable. See tmpnam (Peterson 1992a) for details.

See Also

ar (CP), as (CP), cc (CP), ld (CP), a.out (F), ar (F), tmpnam (Peterson 1992a)

Object Files chapter (AT&T 1990g)

nm (CP)   OBJECT FILE MANIPULATION   nm (CP)

Name

nm—display the symbol table of common object file(s)

Synopsis

nm [−*VTefhlnopruvx*] *filename* . . .

Description

nm prints the symbol table of each specified COFF or ELF file. The file may be an archive(s) of relocatable or absolute COFF or ELF files, or it may be a relocatable or absolute COFF or ELF file.

Symbol Table Information

The following information is printed for each symbol:

Index specifies the index (in brackets) of the symbol.

Value gives the symbol value, expressed as a virtual address (in executable and dynamic library files), or as a section offset (for symbols defined in a relocatable file), or as alignment constraints (for symbols that have SHN __COMMON as a section index.

Size gives the symbol's size in bytes if the information is available.

Type gives the symbol's type and derived type. The type may be one of the following:

FILE is the type if the symbol is the name of a source file.

FUNC is the type if the symbol is function or some other executable code.

NOTYPE is the type if no type was specified.

OBJECT is the type if the symbol is data object such as an array or variable.

SECTION is the type if the symbol is a section symbol.

Bind specifies the symbol's binding attributes, which may be as follows:

GLOBAL symbols are visible in each object file of a combined set of object files.

LOCAL symbols have a scope that is limited to the object file which contains their definition.

WEAK symbols are global symbols that have a lower precedence than GLOBAL symbols.

Other is a field which is reserved for future use. It now contains 0.

Shndx is (except for three special values below) the section header table index for a symbol. The special values are as follows:

ABS indicates that the value of the symbol will not change because of relocation.

COMMON indicates that a block is unallocated and that the symbol value specifies alignment restraint.

UNDEF indicates a symbol that is not defined.

Name gives the name of the symbol.

Diagnostic Messages

"nm: *name*: cannot open" means that *name* cannot be read.

"nm: *name*: bad magic" means that *name* is not a commom object file.

"nm: *name*: no symbols" means that symbols have been stripped from *name*.

Options and Arguments

Obsolete Options

The following options are obsolete and will be removed from a future release:

−e suppresses printing of all symbols except external and static symbols.

Automatic symbols can appear in the debugging information that is produced by cc −g, but they no longer can appear in the symbol table.

−f causes full output to be displayed. Redundant symbols (e.g., .text or .data) normally suppressed are printed.

−T causes nm to truncate every word that would otherwise overflow its column. It also marks the truncation with an asterisk in the last character position of the column. The default is that nm displays the entire name. If the name is too long to fit, it forces columns to its right to move farther to the right, misaligning columns.

Current Options

The following options may be used singly or in combination, in any order. They may appear anywhere on the command line. Whenever conflicting options are specified (e.g., nm −n −v), the first option is used and the second causes a warning message but is otherwise ignored.

−h suppresses the display of output heading data.

−l appends * to the keyletter for WEAK symbols in order to distinguish such symbols from GLOBAL symbols.

−n sorts external symbols before printing them.

−o uses octal, not hex, to report the size and value of symbols.

−p creates terse, easily parsable output by preceding every symbol with its value (blank if the symbol is undefined) and a type keyletter. The type keyletters are as follows: D (data object symbol), F (file symbol), N (no symbol), S (section symbol), T (text symbol), and U (undefined). If the binding attribute (see bind above) of the symbol is WEAK, the keyletter is printed in uppercase; in addition, the keyletter is preceded by * if −l is specified (see −l and bind) and the binding attribute is WEAK. If the binding attribute is LOCAL, the keyletter is printed in lowercase. If the binding attribute is GLOBAL, the keyletter is printed in uppercase.

−r starts each output line with the name of the object file or archive.

−V prints (on standard output) the version of the nm command being executed.

−v sorts external symbols by value before they are displayed.

−u displays only undefined symbols.

−x reports the size and value of each symbol in hexadecimal rather than in decimal.

Files

TMPDIR/* contains temporary files.

TMPDIR ordinarily is /var/tmp. However, it can be redefined by changing the TMPDIR environment variable. See tmpnam (Peterson 1992a).

See Also

as (CP), cc (CP), dump (CP), ld (CP), a.out (F), ar (F), tmpnam (Peterson 1992a)

prof (CP)	PROFILING	prof (CP)

Name

prof—display profile data produced by the *monitor* function

Synopsis

prof [-a|c|n|t] [-o|x] [-g|l] [-z] [-h] [-s] [-m *mondata*] V[prg]

Description

prof interprets a profile file to create a report that shows the amount of execution time spent in different parts of a program and the number of times each function is called.

In order to profile a program, the program must first be compiled using the -p (profile) option of cc (CP), the compiler. This adds code to each subroutine to count the number of times it is called. Code is inserted that generates calls to monitor (Peterson 1992a), a system routine. Later, when the program is executed, monitor watches program execution and creates a file mon.out (the default name), containing subroutine execution counts that prof later interprets. (It is best to run a program immediately before profiling it to avoid using an old mon.out file by mistake.)

The symbol table in the object file *prg* (the default is a.out) is correlated with the profile file (the default is mon.out). For each external text symbol in the program, prof calculates the percentage of execution time spent executing between that text symbol and the next, together with the number of times the function was called and the average number of seconds per call. Any single function may be split into subfunctions for profiling by using the MARK macro. See prof (AT&T 1990m) for more details.

The -p option of cc causes calls to monitor to be inserted at the beginning and end of execution of programs that call exit (CP) or that return from main. The call to monitor at the end of execution causes the system to create a profile file. Programs that do not explicitly call exit or return from main require a final call to monitor to be coded explicitly. If the -p option was used when a file was compiled, the number of calls to a function is tallied.

The environment variable PROFDIR establishes the name of the profile file created by a program. If PROFDIR is null, no profile data are created. If

PROFDIR doesn't exist, the file mon.out is created in the directory current when the program terminates. If PROFDIR = *string*, then *string*/ *pid.prgname* is created. Here *prgname* is arg[ ] with any path prefix deleted; *pid* is the process ID of *prgname*.

Although prof makes a precise count of the number of function calls, the times reported in successive runs may vary by more than 20 percent. Hidden background processes or asynchronous processes, as well as normal processes, may cause a varying cache hit rate because the program being profiled is sharing the cache with these other processes.

Care must be taken in profiling dynamically linked executables. Because shared objects cannot now be profiled with prof, only the "main" portion of the image of a dynamically linked program is sampled. Time spent in the shared object, i.e., outside the "main" object, will not be shown in the profile summary. Thus, the total program time reported may be less than the total time used. Try to link a program statically before profiling it. Use archives as much as possible when profiling a program.

The prof command creates a display with columns having the following meanings:

name reports which symbols were monitored.

%time reports the percentage of total program run time spent executing each function.

cumsecs reports the cumulative seconds spent executing each function.

#call reports the number of times each function was called during program execution.

ms/call reports the number of milliseconds used by each function call.

Options and Arguments

The options −a, −c, −n, and −t are mutually exclusive; −g and −l are mutually exclusive; and −o and −x are mutually exclusive. Otherwise, the remaining options may be used in any combination.

Sort prof Output Lines

If more than one of the options −a, −c, −n, −t is specified, prof issues a warning and uses only the last option specified.

−a sorts lines by symbol address (increasing).

−c sorts lines by number of calls (decreasing).

−n sorts lines by symbol names (lexically).

−t sorts lines by decreasing percentage of total time (the default option).

Print Symbol Addresses and Symbol Names

−o prints the address (octal) and name of each symbol.

−x prints the address (hex) and name of each symbol.

Choose the Types of Symbols to Report

−g includes static (nonglobal) functions. Unless this option is used, times for static functions are attributed to the most recent external text symbol. The number of calls of the preceding external function is correct in either case, i.e., the call counts for static functions are not added to the call counts for external functions in either case.

−l excludes static (nonglobal) functions (the default option). The −l option adds the time spent in executing a static function to the global function preceding it in memory instead of giving the static function a separate report entry. The resulting report may be misleading unless all static functions are properly located. For example, suppose that functions a( ) and b( ) both are global functions and that b( ) follows a( ) in memory. Suppose further that a( ) is the only one of these two global functions that calls s( ), a static function. If s( ) is properly located, i.e., if s( ) immediately follows a( ), and −l is specified, the amount of execution time spent in a( ) can be ascertained, including the time spent in s( ). On the other hand, if both a( ) and b( ) call s( ), any time spent in executing b( )'s call to s( ) will be attributed to a( ). In this example, s( ) cannot be properly located.

Manipulate the prof *Report*

−h suppresses the profile report heading.

−s prints (on standard error output) a summary of some monitoring parameters and statistics.

Miscellaneous Options

−m *mondata* uses *mondata* as the profile input file, not mon.out.

−V prints prof version information on the standard error output.

−z includes symbols in the profile range that are never called and have zero time.

prg is the object file whose symbol table is to be displayed.

Files

mon.out contains profile data.
a.out contains the symbol table.

See Also

cc (CP), exit (CP), lprof (CP), profil (CP), monitor (Peterson 1992a), prof (AT&T 1990m)
lprof chapter (AT&T 1990g)

prs (CP)   **SOURCE CODE CONTROL SYSTEM**   **prs (CP)**

Name

prs—print an SCCS file

Synopsis

prs [-d[dataspec]] [-r[SID]] [-e] [-l] [-c [yy[mm[dd[hh [mm[ss]]]]]]] [-a] *filenames*

Description

prs is one of a group of 14 commands used to keep track of files as the files evolve through various versions. It prints all or part of one or more .s-files (SCCS files) on the standard output in a format supplied by the user. The data keywords below specify which parts of an .s-file should be retrieved and printed. Every part of an SCCS file has a data keyword associated with it.

prs prints user-supplied text and values extracted from the SCCS file and substituted for data keywords in the order in which they appear in *dataspec*. User-supplied text is text other than a data keyword.

Any data keyword value has either a simple (s) format, in which keywords are directly substituted, or a multiline (m) format, in which a carriage return follows each substitution.

\t specifies a tab and \n specifies the carriage return/newline pair.

Table 1-8 shows the default data keywords in the delta table section of a file.

The default data keywords in the User Names section of the SCCS file are as follows:

Keyword	Data Item	Format	Value
:UN:	names of users	m	*text*

Table 1-9 shows the default data keywords in the flags section of the file.

The default data keywords in the Comments section of the SCCS file are as follows:

Keyword	Data Item	Format	Value
:FD:	file description	m	*text*

TABLE 1-8.   Default data keywords in delta table section of file

Keyword	Data Item	Format	Value
:Dt:	delta information	s	See note
:DL:	delta line statistics	s	:Li:/:Ld:/:Lu:
:Li:	lines inserted	s	*nnnnn*
:Ld:	lines deleted	s	*nnnnn*
:Lu:	lines not changed	s	*nnnnn*
:DT:	delta type	s	*D* or *R*
:I:	SCCS ID string	s	:R:.:L:.:B:.:S:
:R:	release number	s	*nnnnn*
:L:	level number	s	*nnnnn*
:B:	branch number	s	*nnnnn*
:S:	sequence number	s	*nnnnn*
:D:	date delta made	s	:Dy:/:Dm:/:Dd:
:Dy:	year delta made	s	*nn*
:Dm:	month delta made	s	*nn*
:Dd:	day delta made	s	*nn*
:T:	time delta made	s	:Th:::Tm:::Ts:
:Th:	hour delta made	s	*nn*
:Tm:	minutes delta made	s	*nn*
:Ts:	seconds delta made	s	*nn*
:P:	programmer ID	s	*logname*
:DS:	delta sequence number	s	*nnnn*
:DP:	seq. no. of preceding delta	s	*nnnn*
:DI:	seq. no. deltas ignore, excl, inc.	s	:Dn:/:Dx:/:Dg:
:Dn:	seq. no. of included deltas	s	:DS: :DS:...
:Dx:	seq. no. of excluded deltas	s	:DS: :DS:...
:Dg:	seq. no. of ignored deltas	s	:DS: :DS:...
:MR:	MR numbers of a delta	m	*text*
:C:	comments for delta	m	*text*

Note: :Dt: = :DT: :I: :D: :T: :P: :DS: :DP:

The default data keywords in the Body section of the SCCS file are as follows:

Keyword	Data Item	Format	Value
:BD:	body	m	*text*
:GB:	body gotten	m	*text*

Table 1-10 shows other default data keywords in the SCCS file.

Options and Arguments

prs arguments may appear in any order, and each argument applies independently to each specified file.

TABLE 1-9.   **Default data keywords in flags section**

Keyword	Data Item	Format	Value
:FL:	flag list	m	*text*
:Y:	module type flag	s	*text*
:MF:	MR validation	s	yes or no
:MP:	MR validation prgm names	s	*text*
:KF:	warning flag—keyword error	s	yes or no
:KV:	keyword validation string	s	*text*
:BF:	branch flag	s	yes or no
:J:	flag for joint edit	s	yes or no
:LK:	releases locked	s	:R:...
:Q:	user-defined keywords	s	*text*
:M:	module name	s	*text*
:FB:	floor boundary	s	:R:
:CB:	ceiling boundary	s	:R:
:Ds:	SID (default)	s	:I:
:ND:	null delta flag	s	yes or no

−a prints information about removed deltas, i.e., delta type = R, and about deltas remaining, delta type = D. See rmdel (CP). The default is to supply information only for the remaining deltas.

−c [*yy*[*mm*[*dd*[*hh*[*mm*[*ss*]]]]]] specifies the delta cutoff date. Individual two-digit parts of the cutoff date may be separated by any number of nonnumeric characters, for example, −c90/06/19 12:00:30. Any units omitted from the specification of time and date default to maximum values. For example, −c9006 is the same as −c900628235959.

−d *dataspec* specifies the output format for data. The *dataspec* argument is a string of SCCS data keywords (see "DESCRIPTION" above), possibly interspersed with user-supplied text. Any data keyword may be repeated in *dataspec* as often as required.

TABLE 1-10.   **Other default data keywords**

Keyword	Data Item	Format	Value
:W:	what (CP) string	s	:Z::M:\t:I:
:A:	what (CP) string	s	:Z::Y: :M: :I::Z:
:Z:	what (CP) string delimiter	s	@(#)
:F:	SCCS filename	s	*text*
:PN:	SCCS file pathname	s	*text*

−e causes output of the delta specified by the −r keyletter and any other deltas created before that delta. See the −c option. Also, see the −1 parameter. If both of these keyletters are used, data keywords are substituted for all deltas of the SCCS file.

−1 causes output of the delta specified by the −r keyletter and any other deltas created after that delta. See the −c keyletter.

−rSID prints the delta that has ID version *SID*. The default is the most recently created delta.

filenames are .s-files (SCCS files) to be printed. If *filenames* specifies a directory, *prs* prints all files in the directory except unreadable files and non-SCCS files (files lacking an .s prefix). If a hyphen (−) is used in place of *filenames*, each line of the standard input is treated as the name of an SCCS file or directory whose contents are to be printed, except that, again, any non-SCCS files or unreadable files are ignored.

Files

/var/tmp/pr?????

See Also

admin (CP), cdc (CP), comb (CP), delta (CP), get (CP), help (CP), rmdel (CP), sact (CP), sccsdiff (CP), unget (CP), val (CP), vc (CP), what (CP), sccsfile (F)

---

regcmp (CP)   **C COMPILATION**   **regcmp (CP)**

Name

regcmp—compile a regular expression

Synopsis

regcmp [-] *files*

Description

regcmp compiles regular expressions in one or more files and places the output in *file.i*. The resulting output is C source code. Compiled regular expressions become extern char vectors so that *file.c* files can be compiled and later loaded, or so that *file.i* files may be #included in

C programs. C programs using such `regcmp` output can use `regex(xyz, line)` to apply the regular expression *xyz* to *line*.

Entries in input files consist of names (C variables) followed by at least one blank followed by at least one regular expression enclosed in double quotes.

The `regcmp` command behaves like `regcmp` (Peterson 1992a), so that it usually is not necessary to call `regcmp` from within a C program. This saves memory and time.

Options and Arguments

— places output in *file.c*.

See Also

`regcmp` (Peterson 1992a)

rmdel (CP)   SOURCE CODE CONTROL SYSTEM   rmdel (CP)

Name

`rmdel`—remove a delta (change) from an SCCS file

Synopsis

`rmdel -rSID filenames`

Description

`rmdel` deletes a specified delta from one or more SCCS files. After a specified delta is deleted, its type indicator in the delta table of the specified SCCS file is changed from delta (D) to removed (R).

The delta to be deleted must be a leaf delta: the most recently created delta on its branch in the delta chain of each specified SCCS file. Also, the specified delta cannot be that of a version which is being edited in order to create a delta, i.e., the specified delta must not appear in any entry of the p-file for the specified SCCS file.

Removing a delta requires the effective user to have write permission in the directory that contains the SCCS file. Also, the real user must be the owner of the SCCS file and its directory or the creator of the delta being deleted.

The specified release cannot be locked. See the −l flag of the `admin` command.

Options and Arguments

−r*SID* specifies the *SID* level of the delta to be removed. The release number of the *SID* must be greater than or equal to the floor and less than or equal to the ceiling. Also, *SID* cannot specify a delta for a version being edited to create a delta. That is, the delta cannot be specified in any existing p-file. Use of −r with rmdel is mandatory.

filenames specifies the SCCS files which are to have deltas removed. If *filenames* specifies a directory, rmdel processes each file in the directory, except that it ignores unreadable files and non-SCCS files (files lacking an s. prefix in the last part of the pathname). If − is the file specifier, rmdel treats each line of the standard input as the name of an SCCS file for it to process. Again, it ignores unreadable files and non-SCCS files.

Files

See the "FILES" subsection of the entry for the get (CP) command for a description of all SCCS files.

x-file is created during delta execution. It is renamed as SCCS file after delta execution. See delta (CP).

z-file is created during delta execution. It is deleted during delta execution. See delta (CP).

See Also

admin (CP), cdc (CP), comb (CP), delta (CP), get (CP), help (CP), prs (CP), sact (CP), sccsdiff (CP), unget (CP), val (CP), vc (CP), what (CP), sccsfile (F)

sact (CP)   SOURCE CODE CONTROL SYSTEM   sact (CP)

Name

sact—announce any impending deltas to an SCCS file

Synopsis

sact *filenames*

Description

sact reports about SCCS files that are being edited, i.e., it announces any impending delta. If get −e is executed without delta subsequently being executed, a delta is impending.

The sact output for each file displays five fields separated by spaces:

Field 1 specifies the *SID* of an already existing delta which will be changed to produce a new delta.

Field 2 specifies the *SID* of the impending delta.

Field 3 contains the logname of the user who is creating the impending delta, i.e., the user who executed `get -e`.

Field 4 shows the `get -e` execution date.

Field 5 shows the time `get -e` was executed.

Options and Argument

filenames is a list of file or directory names. If *filenames* specifies a directory, each file in the directory is processed by `sact`, except that `sact` ignores unreadable files and non-SCCS files (files lacking an `s.` prefix in the last part of the pathname). If `-` is the file specifier, each line of the standard input is treated as the name of an SCCS file for `sact` to process. Again, unreadable files and non-SCCS files are ignored.

Files

See the "FILES" subsection of the entry for the `get` (CP) command for a description of all SCCS files.

See Also

`admin` (CP), `cdc` (CP), `comb` (CP), `delta` (CP), `diff` (AT&T 1990q), `get` (CP), `help` (CP), `prs` (CP), `rmdel` (CP), `sccsdiff` (CP), `unget` (CP), `val` (CP), `vc` (CP), `what` (CP)

sccsdiff (CP) SOURCE CODE CONTROL SYSTEM sccsdiff (CP)

Name

`sccsdiff`—compare versions of an SCCS file

Synopsis

`sccsdiff -rSID1 -rSID2` [-p] [-sn] *filenames*

Description

`sccsdiff` compares two versions of an SCCS file and prints (on standard output) any differences found.

Options and Arguments

The options below apply to each specified file. Options other than `-r` are passed to `pr` (CP), which prints any differences found.

-p pipes output for each file through pr (AT&T 1990q).

-rSID1 and -rSID2 specify deltas of an SCCS file to be compared. The two delta versions are passed to bdiff (AT&T 1990q) in the order specified.

-sn specifies the file segment size, n, that bdiff (AT&T 1990q) passes to diff (AT&T 1990q). Use this option if diff fails because of a too-large system load.

filenames may be any SCCS files and any number may be specified.

Files

See the "FILES" subsection of the entry for the get (CP) command for a description of all SCCS files.

/var/tmp/get????? contains temporary files.

See Also

admin (CP), cdc (CP), comb (CP), delta (CP), diff (AT&T 1990q), get (CP), help (CP), prs (CP), rmdel (CP), sact (CP), sccsdiff (CP), unget (CP), val (CP), vc (CP), what (CP), bdiff (AT&T 1990q), pr (AT&T 1990q)

---

sdb (CP)	DEBUGGING	sdb (CP)

Name

sdb—call a symbolic debugger

Synopsis

sdb [-e][-s signum][-V][-W][-w] [objfile [corfile [dirlist]]]

Description

sdb is a symbolic debugger that provides a controlled environment for executing C source programs and examining their core image files and object files. The options used with the sdb command are described near the end of this entry.

When sdb is executed, it displays a prompt, after which any of the symbolic debugger commands described under "Symbolic Debugger Commands" below may be used.

Variables and Procedures

Data stored in text sections cannot be distinguished from functions.

The sdb command writes variable names as they are written in C programs. It does not truncate names. Variables that are local to a procedure may be accessed by using the following form: *procedure: variable.*

If no procedure name is given, the default procedure is the one that contains the current line. If no procedure or file is given, the default file is the current file.

Line Numbers

Line numbers in a source program are referred to as either *filename: number* or *procedure:number.* Whichever it is, the line number is relative to the beginning of the file and *number* corresponds to the line number in the output of pr (AT&T 1990q). If no number is specified, the first line of the specified procedure or file is the line number used. A line number specified without a *filename* or *procedure* denotes a line in the current file.

Line number information in functions that have been optimized cannot be relied upon. Also, information may be missing after optimization.

Arrays

The elements of a multidimensional array may be referred to by either of two forms: *variable[number][number]* ... or *variable[number, number, ...].* The form *number;number* can be used instead of *number* to specify a range of values. An asterisk used in the form *variable[*]* indicates all the values that a subscript is permitted to have. Subscripts may be omitted if they are the last of multiple subscripts specified. If trailing subscripts are omitted, all values of an array or specified subsection of an array are displayed. If all subscripts are omitted, only the address of an array or specified subsection of an array is displayed.

Structures

sdb ordinarily interprets a structure name as a set of variables. Accordingly, sdb displays all the elements of a structure when it is required to display a structure, except when displaying structure addresses. In this case, sdb displays the address of the structure instead of the addresses of individual elements.

The form *pointer[number]* is used for dereferencing pointers. Pointers to structure members are of the form *variable->member; variable* is the address of a pointer. Structure members may be referred to by using the form *variable.member; variable* is the address of an instance of the structure. Combinations of the preceding forms may be used. A number may be substituted for a structure variable name. If substituted, the number is interpreted as the address of the structure and the structure template is that of the last structure referred to by sdb.

Stacks

A given instance of a variable on the stack may be referred to using the following form: *procedure*: *variable, number*. Any naming variation described in the subsection on variables may be used in referring to stack variables. In the above form, *number* refers to the *n*th occurrence of a specified procedure in the stack, counting down from the top, or most current, procedure. If no procedure is given, the currently executing file or procedure is used, i.e., the procedure containing the curent line.

Addresses

Addresses may be used to specify variables. Any integer constant valid in the C language may be used as an address. Thus, addresses may be input in decimal, hexadecimal, or octal.

When a process is executing under *sdb*, every address refers to the address of the executing process. Otherwise, every address refers to either *corfile* or *objfile* (see the description of these two files in the "OPTIONS AND ARGUMENTS" section below; also see argument −w).

All appropriate values of addresses are signed 32-bit numbers so that sdb may be used on large files.

An address mapping for each file determines the address in that file that is associated with a written address. Two vectors represent each mapping: (*b1*, *e1*, *f1*) and (*b2*, *e2*, *f2*). Initial values of the vectors, (*b1*, *e1*, *f1*) and (*b2*, *e2*, *f2*), are suitable for a.out files and core files. If one of the files is not the expected kind, *e1* is set to the maximum file size, while *b1* and *f1* are each set to 0, permitting the whole file to be examined without address translation.

The *fileaddress* that corresponds to a written address is determined as follows: If *b1* is less than or equal to *address* and *address* is less than *e1*, then *fileaddress* equals *address* + *f1-b1*. Otherwise, if *b2* is less than or equal to *address* and *address* is less than *e2*, then *fileaddress* is equal to *address* + *f2-b2*. If neither of these two relations is true, the requested *address* is not allowed.

The two specified segments, (*b1*, *e1*, *f1*) and (*b2*, *e2*, *f2*), may overlap in a few cases, as with programs having separated D and I space.

Symbolic Debugger Commands

The sh (AT&T 1990q) metacharacters * and ? provide pattern matching when used within procedure or variable names in the commands below. There are four places in which sdb cannot handle metacharacters: in file names, as a function name in a line number when sdb is setting a breakpoint, as the argument of the e command, or in the function call command.

If a procedure name is provided, only variables local to the procedure are matched. If a procedure name is not provided, global variables and variables local to the current procedure are matched. The form :*pattern* finds matching global variables only. The form *.* matches all variables.

Controlling Source Program Execution

address:m *count* single-steps through instructions until *address* gets a new value. The count is infinite if *count* is omitted.

B prints a list of breakpoints that are currently active.

count R runs the source program, using no arguments. See *count* r *args*.

count r *args* runs the source program, using the specified arguments. If none is specified, previously used arguments to the program are reused. An argument preceded by < or > redirects the standard input or output, respectively. Full sh syntax is permitted.

If *count* is specified in either of the two preceding commands, it shows the number of breakpoints to be ignored.

D deletes every breakpoint.

I *count* single-steps through *count* machine-language instructions, reactivating the signal that caused execution to stop.

i *count* single-steps through *count* machine-language instructions, not reactivating the signal that caused execution to stop.

k kills the program being debugged.

l prints the last line executed.

level v turns off verbose mode used in single-stepping with m, S, or s if v is specified. Otherwise, the reporting mode is verbose. If verbose mode is specified, *level* determines how verbose the reporting is. If *level* is omitted, the name of the current source file and/or the subroutine name is reported if either one changes. Each C source line is printed before execution if *level* is 1 or more. Each assembler statement is printed if *level* is 2 or more.

linenumber a stands for "announce." The command, in effect, executes *linenumber*:b l; c if *linenumber* is *proc:number*. If *number* is omitted from *proc:number*, the command, in effect, executes *proc*:b T; c.

linenumber b *commands* sets a breakpoint at *linenumber*. If *commands* are omitted, execution stops before the breakpoint; control is handed back to sdb. Otherwise, *commands* are executed when the breakpoint is found, and execution resumes. Control returns to sdb instead of continuing execution if k is executed as the *command*. If a procedure name is given but no *linenumber* (for example, proc:), a breakpoint is put at the first line of the procedure, even if it was compiled without using the −g option. If *linenumber* is omitted, sdb places a breakpoint at the current line. Multiple commands may be specified by separating them with semicolons. Associated commands cannot be nested.

linenumber C *count* continues program execution after a breakpoint or interrupt. The signal which caused the program execution to cease is reactivated. See *linenumber* c *count*.

linenumber c *count* continues program execution after a breakpoint or interrupt. The signal which caused the program execution to cease is not reactivated.

For either of the two preceding commands, if *linenumber* is specified, a temporary breakpoint is placed at the line and execution resumes. The breakpoint is removed when *sdb* finishes. Also, if *count* is specified, execution ceases when *count* breakpoints have been found.

linenumber d removes the breakpoint at *linenumber*. If *line number* is omitted, breakpoints are removed interactively. The location of each breakpoint is displayed and a line is read from standard input. If a line from standard input starts with d or y, the breakpoint is removed.

linenumber g *count* continues program execution after a breakpoint, resuming execution at the specified *linenumber*. The number of breakpoints to be ignored is specified by *count*.

procedure(*arg1*, *arg2*, . . .) prints the value returned by the procedure according to the the default format, d.

procedure(*arg1*, *arg2*, . . .)/*m* prints the value returned by the procedure according to the format specified by *m*. The default format is d.

Each of the two preceding commands executes the specified procedure with the arguments given. These may be characters, register names, integers, string constants, or names of variables accessible from the current procedure. Executing this command requires the program to have been compiled using the −g option.

S *count* executes the program by single-stepping through *count* lines. It will not step into a called function. Instead, it steps over such a function.

s *count* executes the program by single steps, stepping through *count* lines and not stepping through procedure calls. s is able to step from one function into a called function.

Either of the two preceding commands executes one line if *count* is not specified.

variable$m *count* single-steps through instructions until *variable* gets a new value. The *variable* must be accessible from the current procedure. The count is infinite if *count* is omitted.

Debugger-Debugging Commands
The following three commands are used in debugging the debugger:
Q prints a list of files and procedures being debugged.

V prints the version number of **sdb**.

Y toggles **sdb** output.

Examining Data in Programs

Commands for examining data in the program are as follows:

linenumber?lm prints (under the control of the format specification *lm*) the value at the address from the executable or text space specified by *linenumber*. The default format is **i**.

linenumber=lm prints (under the control of the format specification *lm*) the address of *linenumber*. The default format specification is **lx** (4 bytes, hex). This command permits conversion between decimal, hexadecimal, and octal.

number=lm prints (under the control of the format specification *lm*) the value of *number*. The default format specification is **lx** (4 bytes, hex). This command converts data between decimal, hexadecimal, and octal.

T prints the top line of a stack trace.

t prints the stack trace of a halted or terminated program. The most recently invoked function is at the top of the stack. At the bottom of the stack is _**start**, the start-up routine that calls **main**, if the program is a C program.

variable!value assigns a *value* (number, character constant, or variable) to *variable*. C language conventions govern any type conversions necessary to make the assignment. Numbers are treated as integers if no exponent or decimal point is used. Otherwise, they are treated as type double variables. Registers other than floating point registers are treated as integers. Register names are the same as those used by the assembler. Character constants are designated by *'character*. Structures are permitted only if a structure variable is being assigned to another structure variable of the same type. The address of *variable* or any variable is treated as having type *int*.

variable/count leng form displays memory. The display is controlled by the values of *variable, count, leng,* and *form* described below. Any of the specifiers, *count, leng,* and *form*, may be omitted. If all are omitted, **sdb** selects a *form* and a *leng* that agree with the type declaration of *variable*.

count (numeric) determines the number of units of memory to be displayed, starting at the address that *variable* implies. If *count* is omitted, characters are printed until a null byte is encountered or until 128 characters are printed.

leng specifies the length of units of memory to be output, using the output format *form*. If *leng* is omitted, the size of a memory unit is equal to the size of *variable*.

A given length specifier may result in truncation of output variables. The possible values of *leng* are as follows:

b   1 byte
h   2 bytes (half a word)
l   4 bytes (a long word)

Any length specifier can be used effectively with the c, d, u, o, and x format specifiers below. The possible format specifiers, *form*, are as follows:

a prints characters, beginning at *variable* '*s* address. Register variables cannot be printed by using this format. If *count* is used with a, that many characters are printed.

c is character.

d is decimal.

f is 32-bit floating point, single precision.

g is 64-bit floating point, double precision.

I disassembles machine-language instructions and prints addresses numerically.

i disassembles machine-language instructions and prints addresses both numerically and symbolically.

o is octal.

p is a pointer to a procedure.

s prints characters starting at the address pointed to by *variable*; s assumes that *variable* is a string pointer. If *count* is used with s, that many characters are printed.

u is decimal, unsigned.

x is hexadecimal.

variable:?*lm* prints (under the control of the format specification *lm*) the value at the address from the executable or text space specified by *variable*. The default format is i.

variable = *lm* prints (under the control of the format specification *lm*) the address of *variable*. The default format specification is 1x (4 bytes, hex). This command permits conversion between decimal, hexadecimal, and octal.

X displays the current machine-language instruction.

x displays the machine registers and the current machine-language instruction.

Examining Source Files

The debugger maintains the variables *current-line* and *current file*. If *corfile* (see *corfile* in the "OPTIONS AND ARGUMENTS" section below) exists, these two variables are initially set to the line and file that contain the source statement at which the process terminated. Otherwise, the two variables are set to indicate the first line of main( ). Some of the following commands can change *current-file* and *current-line*:

/regular expression/ searches forward from the current line, looking for a line containing a string that matches *regular expression*. See *ed* (AT&T 1990q). The trailing */* may be omitted, except when it is associated with a breakpoint.

?regular expression? searches backward from the current line, looking for a line containing a string that matches *regular expression*. See *ed*. The trailing *?* may be omitted, except when it is associated with a breakpoint.

count+ advances by *count* lines to the new current line and prints the new current line.

count– retreats by *count* lines to the new current line and prints the new current line.

e prints the name of the current file.

e directory/ adds *directory* to the end of the list of directories.

e filename makes *filename* the current source file. The first line of the specified procedure or file becomes the current line.

e procedure makes the file that contains *procedure* the current source file.

For each of the four preceding *sdb* commands, the first line of the new file becomes the current line. If no procedure, filename, or directory is specified, the current values of the procedure, filename, or directory are displayed.

number sets the current line to line *number* and prints the new line.

p prints the current line.

z prints the current line and the following nine lines. The last line printed becomes the new current line.

w prints a window consisting of the 10 lines surrounding the current line.

Miscellaneous Commands

!command causes *command* to be passed to *sh* (AT&T 1990q), the shell, where it is interpreted.

"string" prints *string*. The command recognizes C escape sequences in *string* like *\character*, *\octaldigits*, or *\hexdigits*, where *character* is nonnumeric. The trailing *"* may be omitted.

./ redisplays the last variable displayed by another command.

< file reads commands from *file* until it encounters an end-of-file character, after which it continues to read commands from standard input. This command may not be nested. Thus *<* may not appear in the file as a command. If a command given in *file* or standard input directs *sdb* to display a variable, the variable name is displayed too. Before being executed, commands are echoed, preceded by two asterisks.

end-of-file character scrolls 10 lines, displaying data, instructions, or the source, depending on which of these was last printed. Control-D usually is the end-of-file character for such scrolling.

M prints address maps.

newline advances the current line by one and prints the new line if the previous line displayed a source line. Otherwise, if a memory location was printed by the previous command, the next memory location is printed. If the previous command disassembled an instruction, *newline* disassembles the next instruction.

q exits sdb.

V prints sdb version stamping information.

Options and Arguments

−e treats any nonsymbolic addresses as offsets and causes symbolic information to be ignored.

−s *signum* can be used more than once on the command line. It causes live processes under the control of sdb not to be stopped when signal number *signum* (decimal) is received signal [see signal (Peterson 1991a)].

−V causes sdb to print version information. sdb will exit after printing such information if no *objfile* argument is specified on the command line.

−W disables warnings (and checking) that otherwise occur when the source files used in producing *objfile* are newer than *objfile* or cannot be found, or when the *corfile* is older than *objfile*.

−w permits addresses in *objfile* or *corfile* to be overwritten.

corfile is a core image file that is generated if *objfile* terminates abnormally or if gcore (AT&T 1990q) is executed. The default name of the core image file is core. If it exists, the core image file contains a copy of segments of the program. sdb can be used even if the core image file does not exist. If − is specified in place of *corfile*, it causes sdb to ignore any core image file. If no *corfile* exists, the current file that sdb initially examines is the file that contains main and the current line number that sdb initially examines is the first line of main. If *corfile* exists, sdb initially sets the current line and current file to the line and file that contain the source statement where the process terminated.

dir-list is a colon-separated list of directories containing the source files used in building *objfile*. sdb searches the current directory for source files if no *dir-list* is specified.

objfile is an executable program file. *objfile* must have been compiled using the −g (debug) option of the compiler in order for the full capabilities of sdb to be used. If −g was not used, sdb still can can be used to examine *objfile* and debug it, though its debugging capabilities will be limited. The default *objfile* is a.out. *objfile* can be a pathname in the /proc directory; in this instance, sdb controls the currently executing process specified by that pathname. When sdb is not examining a live process, all addresses and identifiers refer to either *objfile* or *corfile*.

If *objfile* is a dynamically linked executable, any shared object in which a variable or function is defined must be attached to the dynamically linked executable before any such variable or function is referenced by the executable.

The PATH variable can be used to access the *objfile* argument for debugging information.

Files

    a.out
    core

See Also

a.out (F), cc (CP), core (F), ed (1990q), gcore (AT&T 1990q), sh (AT&T 1990q), signal (Peterson 1991a).
sdb chapter (AT&T 1990g)

size (CP)	OJBECT FILE MANIPULATION	size (CP)

Name

size—print the section size of common object files

Synopsis

size [-n] [-f] [-o] [-x] [-V] *filenames*

Description

size prints either segment or section size information (in bytes) for each loaded section of the specified COFF or ELF object file(s). size reports the size of the text (executable code), data (initialized data), and the bss (uninitialized data) segments or sections and their total size. However, since the size of the bss section is unknown until link time, size does not report the true size of objects before linking takes place.

Archive files may be input to size. This creates a size report for all archive members. size prints segment or section sizes for COFF or ELF files entered on its command line.

size tries to calculate segment information: the total file size of nonwritable segments, the total file size of writable segments, and the total memory size of writable segments less the total file size of all writable segments. However, if size cannot calculate segment information, it calculates section information:

the total size of sections that are allocatable, nonwritable, and not NOBITS; the total size of sections that are allocatable, writable, and not NOBITS; and the total size of writable sections whose type is NOBITS. NOBITS sections take up no space in *filenames*.

Options and Arguments

-F prints the size and permission flags of each loadable segment and the total size of all loadable segments. size prints an error message and ceases processing if there are no section data.

-f prints the size and name of each allocatable section, as well as the total size of all allocatable sections. size prints an error message and ceases processing if there are no section data.

-n prints the memory size of each loadable segment or the file size of each nonloadable segment, as well as the permission flags and total size of all segments if segment data exist. If no segment data exist, size prints the memory size and section name of each allocatable and nonallocatable section, as well as the total size of all sections. size prints an error message and ceases processing if there are neither segment nor section data.

-o prints size numbers in octal instead of decimal.

-V prints version information for the size command.

-x prints size numbers in hexadecimal instead of decimal.

filenames is a.out by default.

See Also

as (CP), cc (CP), ld (CP), a.out (F), ar (F)

strip (CP)   **OBJECT FILE MANIPULATION**   **strip (CP)**

Name

strip—strip the symbol table and line numbers from the file(s)

Synopsis

strip [-l] [-x] [-b] [-r] [-V] *filename* . . .

Description

strip strips symbol table, line number information (relocation bits), and debugging information from specified ELF files. This reduces the file storage overhead used by an object file. It is no longer possible to strip COFF files.

Once a file is stripped, the sdb command can no longer be used on the file. Thus strip is useful for preparing production modules after debugging and testing is finished.

After strip is executed, the number of characters reported by −ls −l differs from the size reported by the size command because, after strip is executed, the file still contains some header information not counted as part of the text, data, or bss sections.

If strip processes a common archive file, it will remove the archive symbol table. Before the archive can be link-edited by ld (CP), the archive symbol table must be restored, using the ar (CP) command with an −s option; strip complains if this restoration is required.

strip will not delete the symbol table section if the section is contained by a segment or if the file is a dynamic shared object or a relocatable object. Also, strip will not delete line number and debugging sections if they are contained by a segment or if the relocation section associated with them is contained by a segment.

Options and Arguments

The options below control the amount of information stripped from the symbol table:

−b leaves static symbol, external symbol, and scoping information unstripped. This option will be removed from the next release; it is obsolete.

−l strips line number information only.

−r leaves static symbol, external symbol, and relocation information unstripped. This option will be removed from the next release; it is obsolete.

−V reports (on standard output) the version number of the strip command being executed.

−x leaves static and external symbol information unstripped. Debugging and line information may be stripped.

filename is the common object file from which symbol table information is to be stripped.

Files

TMPDIR/strp* contains temporary files
TMPDIR ordinarily is /var/tmp. It can redefined by changing the environment variable TMPDIR. See tmpnam (AT&T 1990q) for additional details.

See Also

ar (CP), as (CP), cc (CP), ld (CP), a.out (F), ar (F), tmpnam (Peterson 1992a),

tsort (CP)   SORTING   tsort (CP)

Name

`tsort`—topological sort

Synopsis

`tsort` [*filename*]

Description

`tsort` generates (on standard output) a totally ordered list. The total ordering of items is consistent with a partial ordering of items in the input file.

The input is pairs of nonempty strings separated by blanks. Pairs of differing items designate the ordering. Pairs of identical items merely indicate presence, not ordering.

Diagnostic Messages

"Odd data: there is an odd number of fields in the input data."

Options and Arguments

filename contains the input to `tsort`. If no *filename* is specified, input comes from the standard input.

See Also

`lorder` (CP)

unget (CP)   SOURCE CODE CONTROL SYSTEM   unget (CP)

Name

`unget`—undo a prior *get* of an SCCS file

Synopsis

`unget` [-r*SID*] [-s] [-n] *filenames*

Description

`unget` reverses the effect of a `get` -c that previously was executed on one or more files. `unget` must be executed by the same user who executed the `get` -e whose effects are to be reversed.

Options and Arguments

The following options affect each named file independently:

$-rSID$ specifies which delta [the SID specified by a previous get CP)] is no longer intended. The $-r$ option need not be specified if only two or more gets by a user (login name) are outstanding on a SCCS file. The unget command will complain if a needed SID is omitted from the command line or if an ambiguous SID is given.

$-s$ suppresses display (on standard output) of the SID of the new delta about to be created.

$-n$ retains file(s) retrieved by get (CP). The default is that the file is removed from the current directory.

filenames specifies the SCCS file(s) which unget is to process. If *filenames* specifies a directory, unget processes each file in the directory, except that unget ignores non-SCCS files and unreadable files. If *filenames* is $-$, each line of standard input is treated as the name of an SCCS file for unget to process.

Files

See the "FILES" subsection of the entry for the get (CP) command for a description of all SCCS files.

p-file
q-file
z-file

See Also

admin (CP), cdc (CP), comb (CP), delta (CP), get (CP), help (CP), prs (CP), rmdel (CP), sact (CP), sccdiff (CP), val (CP), vc (CP), what (CP)

---

val (CP)   SOURCE CODE CONTROL SYSTEM   val (CP)

Name

val—validate an SCCS file

Synopsis

```
val -
val [-s] [-rSID] [-mname] [-ytype] filenames
```

Description

val determines if a specified file is an SCCS file with characteristics matching those specified by the optional argument list.

val returns an 8-bit error code upon exit. Since multiple files may be specified on a val command line, and since val can process multiple command lines, val returns a logical OR of the code created for each file and command line it processes. A return code of zero means that every file matched the specified characteristics.

Each bit set in an individual 8-bit error code indicates a specific error. Set bits are interpreted as follows, moving from left to right:

Bit 0 set means that a file argument is missing.

Bit 1 set means that a keyletter is unknown or duplicated.

Bit 2 set means that an SCCS file is corrupted.

Bit 3 set means that a file is not SCCS or cannot be opened.

Bit 4 set means that an *SID* is invalid or ambiguous.

Bit 5 set means that an *SID* is nonexistent.

Bit 6 set means a %Y%, −y mismatch.

Bit 7 set means a %M%, −m mismatch.

Options and Arguments

The effects of the following keyletter arguments apply independently to each file specified. The keyletter arguments may appear in any order.

− causes the standard input to be read until an end-of-file condition (CTRL-D) is detected. Each line of standard input is processed independently, as if it were a separate command list. This allows one val to have different values for options and filenames. The − option is treated differently by val than by other SCCS commands. Also, it is not used with other options of val.

−m*name* compares the value of *name* with the SCCS %M% keyword in *filenames*, i.e., the value of *name* is compared with the value set by the −m flag of admin (CP).

−r*SID* determines whether the specified *SID* is ambiguous or invalid. An *SID* is ambiguous if it does not physically exist but implies one which may exist. For example, −r1 does not exist but implies 1.2, which may exist. An *SID* is invalid if it cannot exist as a valid *SID* number, for example, r1.1.0. If the *SID* is neither ambiguous nor invalid, val determines whether it exists.

−s suppresses diagnostic messages. Such messages are otherwise sent to the standard output file for any error found while processing each file listed on each command line.

−y*type* compares the value of *type* with the SCCS %Y% keyword in *filenames*, i.e., the value of *type* is compared with the value set by the −t flag of admin (CP).

filenames specifies SCCS files to be processed by val. Up to 50 files can be specified on a val command line.

Files

See the "FILES" subsection of the entry for the get (CP) command for a description of all SCCS files.

See Also

admin (CP), cdc (CP), comb (CP), delta (CP), get (CP), help (CP), prs (CP), rmdel (CP), sact (CP), sccsdiff (CP), unget (CP), vc (CP), what (CP)

vc (CP)	SOURCE CODE CONTROL SYSTEM	vc (CP)

Name

vc—version control copies lines from input to output

Synopsis

vc [-a] [-t] [-c*char*] [-s] [*keyword*= *value* . . . *keyword* = *value*]

Description

vc will be removed from the next System V release because it is obsolete.

vc copies lines from standard input to standard output. Command line options and control statement conditions present in standard input jointly control this output.

During copying, the command may replace user-defined keywords(s) appearing in plain text or in control words in standard input with their string *value*. A keyword consists of up to 9 alphanumeric characters, of which the first must be alphabetic. An acceptable value to assign to a keyword is any ASCII string, including numeric values, that ed (AT&T 1990q) can create, except that no blanks or tabs may be embedded. A numeric value is any unsigned string of digits. If an uninterpreted control character is preceded by a \, it can be included in a value. Also, a literal \ can be included in a value by preceding it with another \.

vc returns 0 after a normal exit and 1 after an error.

Version Control Statements

Replacement of keywords by values occurs if a keyword enclosed by control characters is found in a version control statement. A control statement consists of one line beginning with a control character, unless the line is modified by the −t option below.

The default control character is a colon (:), but see the −c option below. Any input lines that begin with a \ followed by a control character are not control lines. Such lines are copied to standard output after the \ is removed. However, lines that begin with a \ that is followed by a control character are copied to standard output without removal of the \.

Version control statements are as follows:

::*text* replaces any keywords that occur in lines copied to the standard output. The two leading control characters :: are deleted, and any keywords enclosed by control characters in *text* are replaced by their assigned values before the line is copied to standard output. The action of this control statement is independent of option −a below.

:asg *keyword*=*value* assigns values to keywords. This overrides assignments made for corresponding keywords on vc's command line and any earlier :asg statements assigning a value to that keyword. Any keywords that are declared without assigning them values have null values assigned to them.

:ctl *char* changes the control character to *char*.

:dcl *keyword*[, . . . *keyword*] declares keywords. Every keyword must be declared.

$$:if\ condition$$

.

.

.

:end copies all lines between the if statement and its matching end statement to the standard output if the if condition is true. Otherwise, all such lines are discarded, including any control statements. Any intervening :if and :end statements are used only to maintain matching of if-end pairs. The syntax of *condition* is described by the following rules:

```
<cond>    ::= [ "not" ] <or>
<or>      ::= <and> | <and> "|" <or>
<and>     ::= <exp> | <exp> "&" <and>
<exp>     ::= "(" <or> ")" | <value> <op> <value>
<op>      ::= "=" | "!=" | "<" | ">"
<value>   ::= <ASCII string> | <numeric string>
```

Each *value* must be separated from any operators or parentheses by at least one blank or tab. The operators are as follows:

=	equal. Operates on strings.
! =	not equal. Operates on strings.
>	greater than. Operates on unsigned integers.
<	less than. Operates on unsigned integers.
&	and. Operates on strings.
|	or. Operates on strings.
( )	logical grouping. May be used to alter precedence.
not	use only after **if**. Inverts the value of *condition*.

The precedence of operators is as follows, from highest to lowest:

$$= \; ! = \; > \; < \qquad \text{all have equal precedence.}$$
$$\&$$
$$|$$

:err *message* prints *message* followed by "ERROR: err statement on line . . . (915)." Afterward, **vc** stops execution and returns an exit code of 1, indicating that an error has occurred.

:msg *message* prints *message* on diagnostic output.

:off turns off keyword replacement for every line.

:on turns on keyword replacement for every line.

Options and Arguments

−a replaces keywords surrounded by control characters with their assigned values in all text lines, in addition to replacing them in **vc** statements.

−c *char* specifies use of *char* as a control character instead of **:**.

−s suppresses warning messages (not error messages) ordinarily displayed on diagnostic output.

−t ignores all characters from the start of a line up to (and including) the first tab character when searching for a control statement. All characters in a control statement up to (and including) the tab are discarded if detected.

Files

See the "FILES" subsection of the entry for the **get** (CP) command for a description of all SCCS files.

See Also

admin (CP), cdc (CP), comb (CP), delta (CP), get (CP), help (CP), prs (CP), rmdel (CP), sact (CP), sccsdiff (CP), unget (CP), vc (CP), what (CP), ed (AT&T 1990m)

---

what (CP)   SOURCE CODE CONTROL SYSTEM   what (CP)

Name

what—identify an SCCS file by searching for a pattern

Synopsis

what [-s] *filenames*

Description

what searches specified files for any occurrences of a special pattern, currently (@(#)), substituted for %Z% by get (CP). It prints text following the pattern until it encounters the first ", null character, >, newline, or \. As an example, if the C program in file.c contains the line

$$\text{char commnt[ ] = "@(#)comments";}$$

and file.c is compiled, yielding file.o and a.out, then if

$$\text{what file.c file.o a.out}$$

is executed, the what command will print

file.c comments
file.o comments
a.out comments

The get command automatically inserts identification information in files. what is intended for use in finding such information, although it can, of course, be used in finding information inserted by other means.

Diagnostic Messages

The command returns 1 if no matches were found. Otherwise, it returns 0.

Options and Arguments

−s causes *what* to quit after it finds the first instance of pattern (@(#)) in each file.

filenames specifies the files to be searched.

Files

See the "FILES" subsection of the entry for the get (CP) command for a description of all SCCS files.

See Also

admin (CP), cdc (CP), comb (CP), delta (CP), get (CP), help (CP), prs (CP), rmdel (CP), sact (CP), sccsdiff (CP), unget (CP), vc (CP), what (CP)

---

yacc (CP)　　　**LEXICAL/SYNTACTIC ANALYSIS**　　　**yacc (CP)**

Name

yacc—yet another compiler-compiler

Synopsis

yacc [−Vvdlt] [−Q[y|n] *filename*

Description

yacc transforms a context-free grammar contained in a specification file into a set of tables for input to a parser which executes an LR(1) parsing operation. The parser, created by yacc, is a finite state machine with a stack.

Each state of the parser has its own integer label. The current state of the parser is always on the top of the stack. The parser can look ahead, reading and remembering the next token in the input (the look-ahead token). The parser starts with only state 0 in the stack and with no look-ahead token having been read.

The parser can perform only four actions: shift, reduce, accept, and error. Using one or another of these actions, the parser makes a single step from one state to another as follows:

It examines its current state and decides if a look-ahead token is required to choose an action. If a look-ahead token is needed, the parser calls yylex to get it.

The current state and the look-ahead token (if required) jointly determine the next action of the parser, possibly causing the look-ahead token to be processed or ignored, or states to be popped off the stack or pushed on.

The shift action is the action the parser most frequently takes. Invariably, a look-ahead token is available when a shift is performed. In some parser state, say 20, there may be an action, say,

IF shift 30

stating that if the look-ahead token is IF, the current state, 20, is pushed down into the stack, and state 30 is put on top of the stack (becomes the current state). The look-ahead token is discarded.

The **reduce** action prevents the stack from growing large without bound. The action goes back to an earlier state of the stack, to a point where the parser first found the right side of a given rule. The parser then acts as if it had seen the left side of the rule at that time.

The **accept** action is taken when the look-ahead token is the end marker. It indicates that the parser has succeeded in examining the entire input, and the input matches the specification.

The **error** action is taken when the parser reaches a point where it cannot continue parsing according to specifications.

The grammar may be ambiguous, i.e., there may be input strings that can be structured in more than one way. Two disambiguating rules are used to remove such ambiguities:

- Do the shift when there is a shift-reduce conflict; and
- Reduce by the earlier grammar rule to resolve a reduce-reduce conflict.

The output file, y.tab.c, produced by *yacc* must be compiled, yielding a program yyparse. This, in turn, must be loaded together with three other programs: main; yylex, the lexical analyzer program; and yyerror, an error-handling routine. These programs must be supplied by the user; yylex can be created by *lex* (CP).

Diagnostic Messages

yacc reports (on standard error) the number of shift-reduce and reduce-reduce conflicts found. It also reports any rules not reachable from the start symbol.

Preprocessor Symbol

If the preprocessor symbol YYDEBUG is nonzero, run-time debugging code is included in y.tab.c. Otherwise, if YYDEBUG is zero, the debugging code is not included.

Options and Arguments

−d creates y.tab.h, a file containing #define statements that associate token names declared by users with token codes assigned by yacc. This lets the token codes be accessed by source files other than y.tab.c.

−l specifies that there will be no #line constructs in the code in y.tab.c. Use this option only after the specification file is debugged.

−Q[y|n] puts yacc version information in y.tab.c if −Qy is specified. The default, −Qn, specifies that no version information will be inserted.

−t compiles run-time debugging (default).

−V prints yacc version information on standard output.

−v creates y.output, a file containing both a description of the parsing tables and a report about any conflicts caused by grammar ambiguities.

filename is a specification file containing rules consisting of chains of definitions and alternate definitions written in Backus-Naur form. The rules are accompanied by C code to be invoked when tokens in the input match the rules. Apart from filename, filenames (y.tab.h, y.tab.c, and y.output) are fixed, permitting only one yacc process to execute in a directory at a time.

FILES

y.output
y.tab.c
y.tab.h contains #defines for token names.
yacc.acts contains temporary files.
yacc.debug contains temporary files.
yacc.tmp contains temporary files.
LIBDIR/yaccpar contains a prototype of a parser C program.
LIBDIR ordinarily contains /usr/ccs/lib.

See Also

lex (CP)
yacc chapter (AT&T 1990g)

Part II

File Formats

Name

intro—introduction to file formats

Description

This section describes formats of various System V files. Header files containing declarations of C structures for use with these files ordinarily can be found in the /usr/include and /usr/include/sys directories. The header files needed with each file are given in the description of each file format. Use the syntax #include <*filename*.h> or #include <sys/ *filename*.h> to include these header files in C programs.

Name

a.out—ELF (Executable and Linking Format) files

Synopsis

#include <elf.h>

Description

The link editor, ld (CP), directs its output to the a.out file by default. If no errors occur during linking, ld processes the a.out file further to make the file executable. The a.out file has the same format as the output file produced by the assembler, as (CP), although the assembler file output file has a different name.

Link Time a.out File Format

a.out has the following components at link time:

ELF Header is at the beginning of the a.out file. It describes the organization of the a.out file. It is the only component of the a.out file that has a fixed position.

Program Header Table is an optional component that tells the system how to generate a process image. If a file is to be used to execute a program (create a process image), the program header table must be present. Relocatable files do not need a program header table.

Sections hold most of the object file information that exists at link time: instructions, data, symbol table, relocation information, and so forth. The a.out file may have one or more sections and the sections may appear in any order.

Section Header Table is an a.out file component that describes the a.out file's sections. The header table must have an entry for each section, giving the section name, section size, and so on. Files that are used during linking must have a section header table. Other object files might or might not have such a table.

Execution Time a.out File Format

a.out has the following components when it is loaded into memory for execution:

ELF Header is at the beginning of the a.out file. It describes the organization of the a.out file. It is the only component of the a.out file that has a fixed position.

Program Header Table is a mandatory component that tells how the process image is to be created.

Segments hold object file information for use at execution time. A segment may contain one or more sections (see above). Three logical segments are created when the a.out file is loaded into memory for execution: the text segment, the data segment, and the stack. The stack is automatically extended whenever this is required. The text segment is not writable by the program. Thus, if other processes are executing the same a.out file, they may share a text segment. The data segment consists of initialized data followed by uninitialized data (uninitialized data are actually set to 0). The data segment begins at the next maximal page boundary beyond the last text address. (The maximal page size is the largest page size supported if the system supports more than one page size.) The data segment is extended by using the brk (Peterson 1991a) system call.

During creation of the process image, the part of the file that holds the end of the text and the beginning of the data may be duplicated. The duplicated text at the beginning of the data is not executed. The operating system duplicates the text in order to load the file into memory in multiples of the actual page size without being forced to realign the beginning of the data section to a page boundary. This causes the first data address to be the sum of the the next maximal page boundary beyond the end of the text plus the remainder formed by dividing the last text address by the maximal page size. No duplication of text is neccesary if the last text address is a multiple of the maximal page size.

Section Header Table is an a.out file component that is optional at execution time although mandatory at link time.

See Also

as (CP), cc (CP), ld (CP), brk (Peterson 1991a), elf (Peterson 1992a), Object Files chapter (AT&T 1990a)

ar (F)   FILE FORMATS   ar (F)

Name

ar—archive file format

Synopsis

```
#include <ar.h>
```

Description

ar, the archive command, combines several files into one file, an archive file. Archives are libraries to be searched by ld (CP), the link editor.

Common format archives can be moved from system to system if ar, the portable archive command, is used.

At the beginning of each archive is the archive magic string. It is defined as follows:

```
#define ARMAG "!<arch>\n /* magic string definition */
#define SARMAG 8            /* length of the magic string */
```

Archive file members follow the archive magic string. A file member header precedes each archive file member. The format of the file member header is as follows:

```
#define ARFMAG "'n" /* header trailer string */

struct ar_hdr
{
```

char ar_name[16]; /* '/' terminated a file member name. If the archive member name fits, arname holds the name, terminated with a slash (/) and padded with blanks on the right. If the member's name does not fit, ar_name holds a slash (/) followed by a decimal number that represents the offset of the name in the archive string table described below. */
char ar_date[12]; /* modification date of file member at the time of its insertion into the archive */
char ar_uid[6]; /* user ID of file member */
char ar_gid[6]; /* group ID of file member */
char ar_mode[8]; /* mode (octal) of file member */
char ar_size[10]; /* size of file member */
char ar_fmag[2]; /* header trailer string */
};

If the archive contains printable files, the archive itself is printable because all of the information in the file member headers is in printable ASCII characters. All numeric information in the headers is stored as decimal numbers, except for ar_mode above which is octal.

There are no empty areas in an archive file. Each archive file member starts on an even byte boundary. If necessary, a newline is inserted between files in order to force files to begin on an even byte. Even so, the size given for the file is the actual size of the file without such file padding.

If an archive contains object files (see a.out) the archive includes an archive symbol table as the first file in the archive. ar automatically creates or updates the symbol table. The link editor, ld, uses the symbol table in order to determine which archive members it must load during link editing.

The name of the archive symbol table is of zero length, i.e., the content of ar_name[0] is '/' and the content of ar_name[1] is ' ' and so on.

The archive symbol table has four-byte "words" that use the following machine-independent encoding, even if the natural byte order of the machine is different. The least significant two digits of an eight-digit hexadecimal number comprise the rightmost of the four bytes. The next least significant two hexadecimal digits comprise the byte to the left of the rightmost byte, and so on. The archive symbol table file has the following contents:

- A four-byte field giving the number of symbols.
- An array of offsets into the archive file. The size of the array is 4 bytes * (the number of symbols). Each offset in the array is associated (in order) with a corresponding name in the name string table (see below). Offsets into the string table begin at zero. Each offset specifies the location of the archive header for the associated symbol.
- The name string table. Its length equals ar_size - 4 bytes * [1 + (the number of symbols)]. The name string table has a null terminated string for each element in the offsets array. Names in the name string table consist of all the defined global symbols found in the common object files contained in the archive.

If the name of an archive member is more than 15 bytes long, then a special archive file member holds a table of file names, with each name followed by a slash (\) and a newline. If this string table member is present, it will precede all normal archive members.

sgetl (Peterson 1992a) and sputl (Peterson 1992a) manipulate the number of symbols and the array of offsets.

The strip (CP) command removes all archive symbol entries from the archive file member header. If the archive is subsequently to be used with the link editor, ld, the archive symbol entries must first be restored by executing the ar (CP) command with −ts options.

See Also

ar (CP), ld (CP), strip (CP), sputl (Peterson 1991a), a.out (F)

core (F)	**FILE FORMATS**	core (F)

Name

core—core image file

Synopsis

None

Description

If a process terminates because it receives a signal, System V writes core (a core image of the process) to the working directory of the process if access controls permit this to be done. If the process has an effective user ID that differs from the real user ID, no core image will be produced.

The size of the core file that a process creates is controllable by the user [see getrlimit (Peterson 1991a).

core contains all of the process information that pertains to debugging: hardware register contents, process data, and process status.

The format of core is specific to the type of object file. COFF executable programs create core files that consist of two parts: a copy of the system's per-user data for the process, including the general registers. The format of this section is defined by the header files <sys/user.h> and <sys/reg.h>. The remaining section of a COFF core image holds the actual contents of process data space.

ELF executable programs yield core files that are ELF files, containing ELF program and file headers [see a.out (F)]. The file header has an e_type field that has type ET_CORE. The program header contains one entry for each loadable and writable segment that was part of the address space of the process, including shared library segments. The core image also contains the contents of the segments.

The ELF core file program header has a NOTE segment that contains entries, each with entry name "CORE," that present the following structures: prstatus_t is defined in <sys/procfs.h>. It holds things of interest to the debugger from the u-area of the operating system: general registers, process ID, reason for stopping, signal disposition, state, and so on. The entry that holds this structure has a NOTE type of 1.

fpregset_t is defined in <sys/regset.h>. It holds the floating point registers. Its NOTE type is 2, and it is present only if the process used floating point registers.

prpsinfo_t is defined in <sys/procfs.h>. It holds information used by the prs (CP) command: controlling terminal, cpu usage, "nice" value, process status, process ID, name of the ELF executable, and so on.

See Also

sdb (CP), getrlimit (Peterson 1991a), setuid (Peterson 1991a), elf (Peterson 1992a), a.out (F), signal (AT&T 1990m), crash (AT&T 1990o), Object Files chapter (AT&T 1990a)

Name

sccsfile—SCCS file format

Synopsis

None

Description

An SCCS (Source Code Control System) file is an ASCII file that has six logical parts: checksum, delta table, user names, flags, comments, and body. Any logical part of an SCCS file may have lines which begin with a control character consisting of an ASCII SOH (start of heading) character (octal 001). Any line in any of the logical parts of an SCCS file that is not shown in the description below as beginning with a control character is prevented from beginning with the control character. File entries of the form *DDDDD* represent a five-digit string—a number between 00000 and 99999.

The six logical parts of an SCCS file are as follows:

Checksum

The checksum is the first line of an SCCS file. It has the following form:

@h*DDDDD*

The value of the checksum is the sum of all characters except the characters in the first line of the SCCS file. @h provides a magic number of 064001 octal, depending on byte order.

Delta table

The delta table contains information about each delta. It has a variable number of entries. Each line in the delta table has one of the following forms:

@s *DDDDD/DDDDD/DDDDD* gives the number of lines inserted, followed by the number of lines deleted, followed by the number of lines left unchanged.

@d <*type*> <*SCCS ID*> *yr/mo/da hr:min:sec* <*pgrmr*> *DDDDD DDDDD* gives the type of delta (D: normal or R: removed), the SCCS ID of the delta, the date and the time of creation of the delta, the login name that corresponds to the real user ID in effect when the delta was created, the serial number of the delta, and the serial number of the preceding delta.

@i *DDDDD* . . . is an optional line that contains the serial numbers of the deltas included.

@x *DDDDD* . . . is an optional line that contains the serial numbers of the deltas excluded.

@g *DDDDD* . . . is an optional line that contains the serial numbers of the deltas that are ignored.

@m *<MR number>* is an optional line which contains one MR number associated with a delta. More than one @m line may appear in an SCCS file.

@c *<comments>* contains comments associated with a delta. More than one @c line may appear in an SCCS file.

@e is a line that ends the delta table entry.

User Names

User names is a list of login names and/or numerical group IDs of users who are permitted to add deltas to the SCCS file. If the list is empty, any user is allowed to make deltas. User names are separated by newlines. Any lines that contain user names and/or numerical group IDs are bracketed by @u and @U lines. If any line starts with a !, it prohibits the following group or user from making deltas.

Flags

Flags give definitions of internal keywords. See **admin** (CP) for additional details. Each flag line has one of the following forms:

@f *<flag>* *<optional text>*

where the following flags and optional text are defined:

t *<program type>* defines the replacement for the %Y% identification keyword.

v *<program name>* controls prompting for MR numbers in addition to comments. If *program name* is present, it specifies the name of a program for checking the validity of MR numbers.

i *<keyword string>* determines whether the "No id keywords" message indicates a warning or a fatal error. If i is present, occurrence of the message indicates a fatal error that causes the file not to be gotten or the delta not to be made. If i is not present, the message is only a warning.

b permits the −b keyletter to be used on the **get** command to cause a branch in the delta tree.

m *<module name>* defines the first choice for text to replace the %M% identification keyword.

f *<floor>* defines the floor release, the release below which no delta may be added.

c <*ceiling*> defines the ceiling release, the release above which no delta may be added.

d <*default* SID> defines the default SID to be used if no SID is specified on a get command.

n makes delta insert a null delta (a delta that does not apply a change) in any releases that are skipped when a delta is made in a new release. For example, if delta 6.1 is made after delta 2.6, releases 3, 4, and 5 are skipped. Any releseases skipped will be completely empty if the n flag is not present.

j makes get permit concurrent edits of the same base SID.

l <*list*> specifies a list of releases that are locked against any editing.

q <*%Q% replacement*> defines the replacement text for the %Q% identification keyword.

z <*reserved*> is used in certain specialized interface programs.

Comments

Comments contain arbitrary text, usually file description information. The text is bracketed by @t and @T lines.

Body

The body consists of text lines intermixed with control lines. Control lines begin with the control character described above. Text lines do not. Any of the following three kinds of control lines may be used:

@I *DDDDD* is an insert line.

@D *DDDDD* is a delete line.

@E *DDDDD* is an end line. The digit string, *DDDDD*, is the serial number that corresponds to the delta for the control line.

See Also

admin (CP), delta (CP), get (CP), prs (CP)

Bibliography

AT&T. 1984. *AT&T Bell Laboratories Technical Journal 63.* No. 8, Part 2. October. Short Hills, New Jersey: Bell Laboratories.

AT&T. 1985. *UNIX System V Interface Definition, Issue 1.* Short Hills, New Jersey: Bell Laboratories.

AT&T. 1988a. *UNIX System V/386 Programmer's Guide.* Englewood Cliffs, New Jersey: Prentice-Hall.

———. 1988b. *UNIX System V/386 User's Guide.* Second Edition. Englewood Cliffs, New Jersey: Prentice-Hall.

———. 1988c. *UNIX System V/386 User's Reference Manual.* Englewood Cliffs, New Jersey: Prentice-Hall.

———. 1989a. *UNIX System V/386 Programmer's Reference Manual.* Englewood Cliffs, New Jersey: Prentice-Hall.

———. 1989b. *UNIX System V/386 System Administrator's Reference Manual.* Englewood Cliffs, New Jersey: Prentice-Hall.

———. 1990a *UNIX System V Release 4 ANSI C Transition Guide.* Englewood Cliffs, New Jersey: Prentice-Hall.

———. 1990b *UNIX System V Release 4 BSD/XENIX Compatibility Guide.* Englewood Cliffs, New Jersey: Prentice-Hall.

———. 1990c *UNIX System V Release 4 Device Driver Interface/Driver-Kernal Interface (DDI/DKI) Reference Manual.* Englewood Cliffs, New Jersey: Prentice-Hall.

————. 1990d *UNIX System V Release 4 Migration Guide*. Englewood Cliffs, New Jersey: Prentice-Hall.

————. 1990e *UNIX System V Release 4 Network User's and Administrator's Guide*. Englewood Cliffs, New Jersey: PrenticeHall.

————. 1990f *UNIX System V Release 4 Product Overview and Master Index*. Englewood Cliffs, New Jersey: Prentice-Hall.

————. 1990g *UNIX System V Release 4 Programmer's Guide: ANSI C and Programming Support Tools*. Englewood Cliffs, New Jersey: Prentice-Hall.

————. 1990h *UNIX System V Release 4 Programmer's Guide: Character User Interface (FMLI and ETI)*. Englewood Cliffs, New Jersey: Prentice-Hall.

————. 1990i *UNIX System V Release 4 Programmer's Guide: Networking Interfaces*. Englewood Cliffs, New Jersey: PrenticeHall.

————. 1990j *UNIX System V Release 4 Programmer's Guide: POSIX Conformance*. Englewood Cliffs, New Jersey: Prentice-Hall.

————. 1990k *UNIX System V Release 4 Programmer's Guide: STREAMS*. Englewood Cliffs, New Jersey: Prentice-Hall.

————. 1990l *UNIX System V Release 4 Programmer's Guide: System Services and Application Packaging Tools*. Englewood Cliffs, New Jersey: Prentice-Hall.

————. 1990m *UNIX System V Release 4 Programmer's Reference Manual*. Englewood Cliffs, New Jersey: Prentice-Hall.

————. 1990n *UNIX System V Release 4 System Administrator's Guide*. Englewood Cliffs, New Jersey: Prentice-Hall.

————. 1990o *UNIX System V Release 4 System Administrator's Reference Manual*. Englewood Cliffs, New Jersey: Prentice-Hall.

————. 1990p *UNIX System V Release 4 User's Guide*. Englewood Cliffs, New Jersey: Prentice-Hall.

————. 1990q *UNIX System V Release 4 User's Reference Manual*. Englewood Cliffs, New Jersey: Prentice-Hall.

Anderson, Bart. *et al*. 1991. *UNIX Communications*. Indianapolis, Indiana: Howard Sams.

Anderson, Gail, & Anderson, Paul. 1986. *The UNIX C Shell Field Guide*. Englewood Cliffs, New Jersey: Prentice-Hall.

Arthur, Lowell. 1986. *UNIX Shell Programming*. New York: John Wiley & Sons.

Bach, Maurice. 1986. *The Design of the UNIX Operating System*. Englewood Cliffs, New Jersey: Prentice-Hall.

Backhurst, Nigel and Davies, Paul. 1987. *Systems Management Under UNIX*. Harrison, New York: Book Clearing House.

Balay, Richard H. 1988. *User's Introduction to UNIX V*. Dubuque, Iowa: Kendall-Hunt Publishing Company.

Banahan, Mark and Rutter, Andy. 1983. *The UNIX Book*. New York: John Wiley and Sons.

Barron, David and Rees, Michael. 1987. *Text Processing with UNIX*. Reading, Massachusetts: Addison-Wesley.

Bell Laboratories. 1978. "UNIX Time-Sharing System." *The Bell System Technical Journal 57*. No. 6, Part 2, July-August.

Bourne, S.R. 1982. *The Unix System*. Reading, Massachusetts: Addison-Wesley.

————. 1986. *The UNIX V Environment*. Reading, Massachusetts: Addison-Wesley.

Brandt, D. Scott. 1990. *Essential Guide to UNIX in Libraries*. West Port, Connecticut: Meckler Corporation.

Brown, Patrick and Muster, John. 1986. *UNIX for People*. Englewood Cliffs, New Jersey: Prentice-Hall.

Budgen, David. 1986. *Making Use of the UNIX Operating System*. Englewood Cliffs, New Jersey: Prentice-Hall.

Burke, Frank. 1987. *UNIX Systems Administration*. San Diego, California: Harcourt Brace Jovanovich.

Byers, R. A. 1985. *Introduction to UNIX System V*. New York: McGraw-Hill Book Company.

Chirlian, Paul M. 1987. *UNIX for the IBM-PC*. Columbus, Ohio: Merrill Publishing Company.

Christian, Kaare. 1988. *UNIX Command Reference Guide-What They Are, How They Work, How to Use Them*. New York: John Wiley & Sons.

————. 1988. *UNIX Dictionary*. New York: John Wiley & Sons.

————. 1988. *The UNIX Operating System*. 2nd edition. New York: John Wiley and Sons.

Clukey, Lee Paul. 1985. *UNIX and XENIX Demystified*. Blue Ridge, Pennsylvania: Tab Books, Inc.

Deikman, Alan. 1988. *UNIX Programming on the 80286-80386*. Blue Ridge, Pennsylvania: Tab Books, Inc.

Dunsmuir, M. R. 1985. *Programming the UNIX System*. New York: Halsted Press Division of John Wiley & Sons, Inc.

Egan, Janet I. and Teixera, Thomas J. 1988. *Guide to Writing a UNIX Device Driver*. New York: John Wiley and Sons.

————. 1988. *Writing a UNIX Device Driver*. New York: John Wiley and Sons.

Farkas, Daniel. 1988. *UNIX for Programmers*. New York: John Wiley and Sons.

————. 1988. *UNIX for Programmers: An Introduction*. New York: John Wiley and Sons.

Felps, Robert. 1991. *Illustrated UNIX*. Plano, Texas: Wordware.

Foxley, Eric. 1985. *UNIX for Super-Users*. Reading, Massachusetts: Addison-Wesley.

Franzosa, Bill (ed.). 1985. *The UNIX System Encyclopedia*. Palo Alto, California: Yates Ventures.

Gauthier, Richard. 1981. *Using the UNIX System*. Englewood Cliffs, New Jersey: Reston Publishing Co.

Gofton. Peter W. *Mastering UNIX Communications*. Alameda, California: Sybex.

Grottola, Michael G. 1991. *The UNIX Audit: Using UNIX to Audit Unix*. New York: McGraw-Hill Book Company.

Holub, Allen I. 1991. *C + C + + Programming With Objects in C*. New York: McGraw-Hill Book Company.

Harbison, Samuel P., and Guy L. Steele, Jr. 1987. *C: A Reference Manual*. 2nd Edition. Englewood Cliffs, New Jersey: Prentice-Hall.

Horspool, Nigel. 1987. *C Programming in the Berkeley UNIX Environment*. Englewood Cliffs, New Jersey: Prentice-Hall.

Kernighan, Brian W., and Rob Pike. 1984. *The UNIX Programming Environment*. Englewood Cliffs, New Jersey: Prentice-Hall.

Kochan, Stephen. 1988. *Programming in C*. Indianapolis, Indiana: Howard Sams.

———. 1990. *UNIX Shell Programming*. Indianapolis, Indiana: Howard Sams.

———. 1989. *UNIX Networking*. Indianapolis, Indiana: Howard Sams.

Lapin, J. P. 1986. *Portable C and UNIX Systems Programming*. Englewood Cliffs, New Jersey: Prentice-Hall.

Lomuto, Ann and Nico Lomuto. 1983. *A UNIX Primer*. Englewood Cliffs, New Jersey: Prentice-Hall.

McNully Development Incorporated. 1986. *UNIX Reference Guide*. Englewood Cliffs, New Jersey: Prentice-Hall.

Mikes, Stephen. *UNIX: Power Use's Guide*. Berkeley, California: Osborne/McGraw-Hill Inc.

Moore, F. Richard. 1985. *Programming in C with a Bit of UNIX*. Englewood Cliffs, New Jersey: Prentice-Hall.

Moore, Jim. 1988. *UNIX: A Minimal Manual*. San Francisco: W. H. Freeman.

Morgan, Rachel, and Henry McGilton. 1987. *Introducing the UNIX System V*. New York: McGraw-Hill Book Company.

———. 1991. *Introducing the UNIX System V 4*. New York: McGraw-Hill Book Company.

Nichols, Joseph, *et al*. 1986. *UNIX Survival Guide*. New York: Holt Rinehart and Winston.

Norton, Peter and Hahn, Harley. 1991. *Peter Norton's Guide to UNIX*. New York: Bantam Books.

Olczak, Anatole. 1985. *The UNIX Reference Guide for System V*. West Lafayette, Indiana: System Publishing Corporation.

O'Reilly & Associates, Inc. 1986, 1987. *UNIX in a Nutshell*. Newton, Massachusetts: O'Reilly & Associates, Inc.

Parker, Tim. 1990. *UNIX Survival Guide*. Reading, Massachusetts: Addison-Wesley.

———. 1991. *Mastering UNIX*. Alameda, California: Sybex.

Parrette, William. 1991. *UNIX for Application Developers*. New York: McGraw-Hill Book Company.

Pasternack, Irene. 1985. *Exploring the UNIX Environment*. New York: Bantam Books.

Peters, James F. 1988. *UNIX Programming: Methods and Tools*. San Diego, California: Harcourt Brace Jovanovich.

Peterson, Baird. 1991a. *UNIX System V System Calls: Programmer's Rapid Reference*. New York: Van Nostrand Reinhold.

Peterson, Baird. 1991b. *XENIX Commands and DOS Cross Development Services*. New York: Van Nostrand Reinhold.

Peterson, Baird. 1992a. *UNIX System V Libraries: Programmer's Rapid Reference*. New York: Van Nostrand Reinhold.

Peterson, Baird. 1992b. *XENIX System Services: Programmer's Rapid Reference*. New York: Van Nostrand Reinhold.

Poole, P. C. and Poole, Nicola. 1986. *Using Unix by Example*. Reading, Massachusetts: Addison-Wesley.

Quaterman, John S., *et al*. 1988. *The Design and Implementation of the 43SBD UNIX Operating System*. Reading, Massachusetts: AddisonWesley.

Rochkind, Marc J. 1957. "The Source Code Control System." *IEEE Transactions on Software Engineering*. December.

————. 1985. *Advanced UNIX Programming*. Englewood Cliffs, New Jersey: Prentice-Hall.

Santa Cruz Operation. 1989a. *SCO UNIX System V/386 Development System: Programmer's Guide*. Santa Cruz, California: The Santa Cruz Operation, Inc.

————. 1989b. *SCO UNIX System V/386 Development System: Programmer's Reference*. Santa Cruz, California: The Santa Cruz Operation, Inc.

————. 1989c. *SCO UNIX System V/386 Development System: Library Guide*. Santa Cruz, California: The Santa Cruz Operation, Inc.

————. 1989d. *SCO UNIX System V/386 Development System: The STREAMS Network Programmer's Guide*. Santa Cruz, California: The Santa Cruz Operation, Inc.

————. 1989e. *SCO UNIX System V/386 Development System: The STREAMS PRIMER*. Santa Cruz, California: The Santa Cruz Operation, Inc.

————. 1989f. *SCO UNIX System V/386 Development System: The STREAMS Programmer's Guide*. Santa Cruz, California: The Santa Cruz Operation, Inc.

————. 1989g. *SCO UNIX System V/386 Operating System: User's Reference*. Santa Cruz, California: The Santa Cruz Operation, Inc.

————. 1989h. *SCO UNIX System V Development System: Programmer's Reference*. Santa Cruz, California: The Santa Cruz Operation, Inc.

————. 1990. *SCO UNIX System V/386 Operating System: Administrator's Reference*. Santa Cruz, California: The Santa Cruz Operation, Inc.

Salama, Ben and Haviland, Keith. 1987. *UNIX System Programming: A Programmer's Guide to Software Development*. Reading, Massachusetts: Addison-Wesley.

Schirmer, C. 1987. *Programming in C for UNIX*. New York: Halsted Press Division of John Wiley & Sons.

Schreiner, Axel and Friedman, H. George, Jr. 1985. *Introduction to Compiler Construction with UNIX*. Englewood Cliffs, New Jersey: Prentice-Hall.

Seyer, Martin and Mills, William. 1986. *DOS UNIX: Becoming a Super User*. Englewood Cliffs, New Jersey: Prentice-Hall.

Shaw, Myril Clement, and Susan Soltis Shaw. 1986. *UNIX And XENIX System V Programmer's Guide*. Blue Ridge Summit, Pennsylvania: Tab Books, Inc.

————. 1986. *UNIX V and XENIX System V: Programmer's Tool Kit*. Blue Ridge, Pennsylvania: Tab Books, Inc.

————. 1987. *UNIX Internals: A Systems Operations Handbook*. Blue Ridge, Pennsylvania: Tab Books, Inc.

Shirota, Y. and Kunii, T. L. *First Book on Unix for Executives*. Berlin; New York: Springer-Verlag.

Silvester, P. P. 1984. *UNIX: An Introduction for Computer Users*. New York: John Wiley & Sons.

————. 1984. *The UNIX System Book*. Berlin; New York: SpringerVerlag.

————. 1988. *The UNIX System Guidebook*. Berlin; New York: SpringerVerlag.

Sobell, Mark. 1991. *Practical Guide to the UNIX System V*. Reading, Massachusetts: Addison-Wesley.

Specialized Systems Consultants Staff. 1984. *UNIX Command Summary (System V)*. Seattle, Washington: Specialized System Consultants, Inc.

————. 1987. *UNIX System V Command Summary*. Seattle, Washington: Specialized System Consultants, Inc.

Strong, Byran and Hosler, Jay. *UNIX for Beginners: A Step-by-Step Introduction*. New York: John Wiley & Sons.

Taylor, A. 1991. *UNIX Guide*. Portland, Oregon: MIS Press.

Thomas, Rebecca and Jean L. Yates. 1982. *A User Guide to the UNIX System*. Berkeley, California: Osborne/McGraw-Hill.

Thomas, Rebecca, Lawrence R. Rogers, and Jean L. Yates. 1986. *Advanced Programmer's Guide to UNIX System V*. Berkeley, California: Osborne/McGraw-Hill.

Todino, Grace and Strang, John. 1987. *Learning the UNIX Operating System*. Newton, Massachusetts: O'Reilly & Associates, Inc.

Topham, D. W. and Trong, H. 1985. *UNIX and Xenix: A Step by Step Approach for Micros*. New York: Brady Computer Books.

Topham, D. W. and Van Truong, Hai. 1986. *The System V Guide: A UNIX & XENIX Tutorial*. New York: Brady Computer Books.

Waite Group. 1987. *UNIX Communications*. Indianapolis, Indiana: Howard Sams.

————. 1987. *UNIX Papers*. Indianapolis, Indiana: Howard Sams.

————. 1983. *UNIX Primer Plus*. Indianapolis, Indiana: Howard Sams.

Waite Group and Martin, Donald. 1987. *UNIX System Bible*. Indianapolis, Indiana: Howard Sams.

————. 1987. *UNIX System V Primer*. Indianapolis, Indiana: Howard Sams.

Walker, Andy. 1984. *The UNIX Environment*. New York: John Wiley & Sons.

Weinberg, Paul N. and Groff, James R. 1988. *Understanding UNIX: A Conceptual Guide*. Carmel, Indiana: Que Corporation.

Western Electric Co. 1985. *UNIX System V Documents*. Greensboro, North Carolina: Western Electric Co.

Whiddett, R. J. *et al.* 1985. *UNIX: A Practical Introduction for Users*. New York: Halsted Press Division of John Wiley & Sons, Inc.

INDEX

135

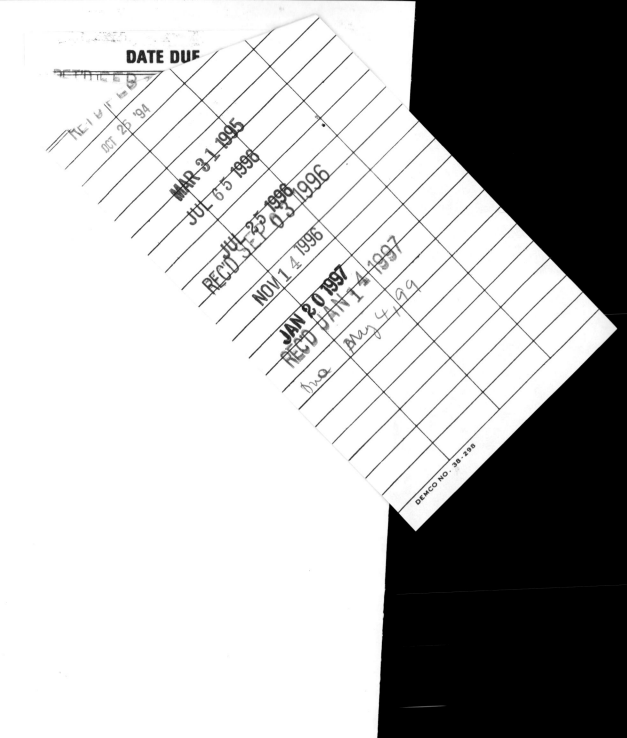